IDW Publishing
San Diego, CA

www.templesmith.com

WORMWOOD™ GENTLEMAN CORPSE
BIRDS, BEES, BLOOD & BEER

created, written & drawn by

Ben Templesmith

letters by

Jason Hanley *(pages 8–28),*
Tom B. Long *(pages 54–75),*
Robbie Robbins *(pages 30–52 and 77–123)*

foreword by

David Slade

edits, charisma and general good looks

Chris Ryall & Dan Taylor

Templesmith logo by Babe Elliot Baker | spiritform.com

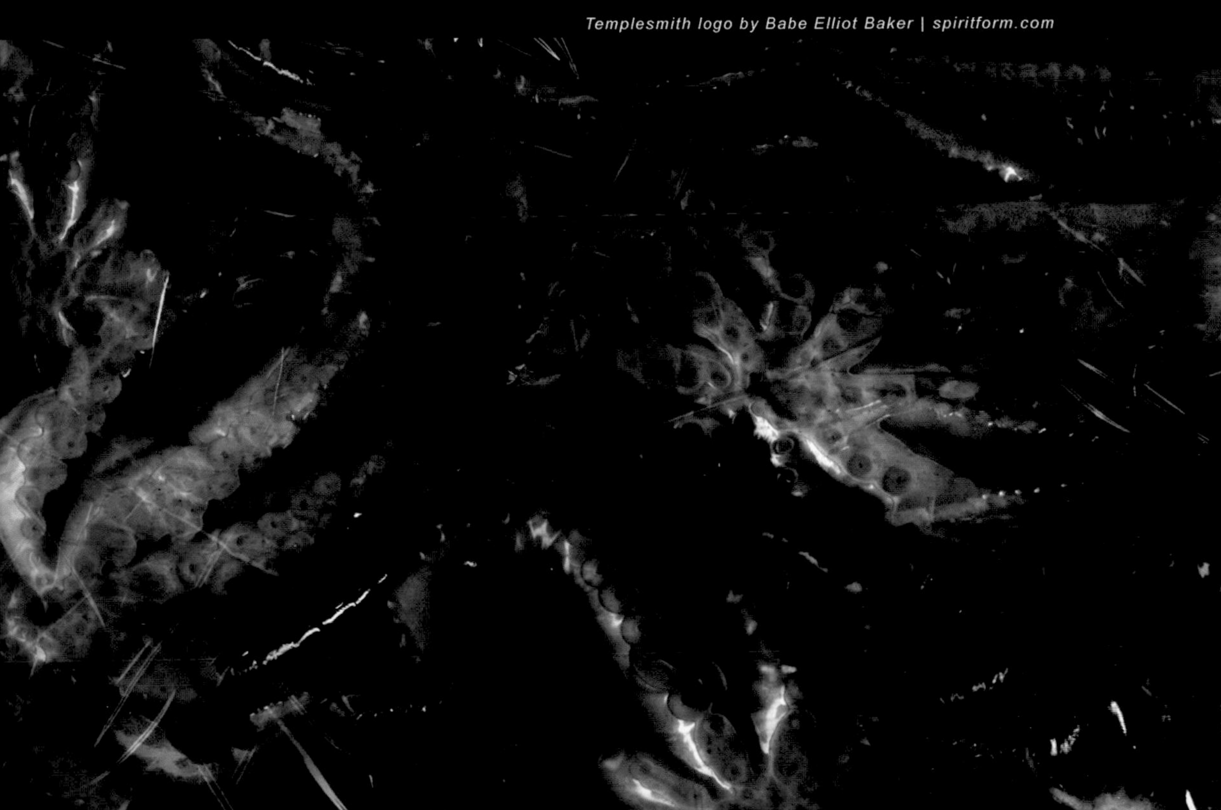

www.IDWPUBLISHING.com ISBN: 978-1-60010-047-5 14 13 12 11 6 7 8 9

Originally published as WORMWOOD: GENTLEMAN CORPSE Issues #0-4.

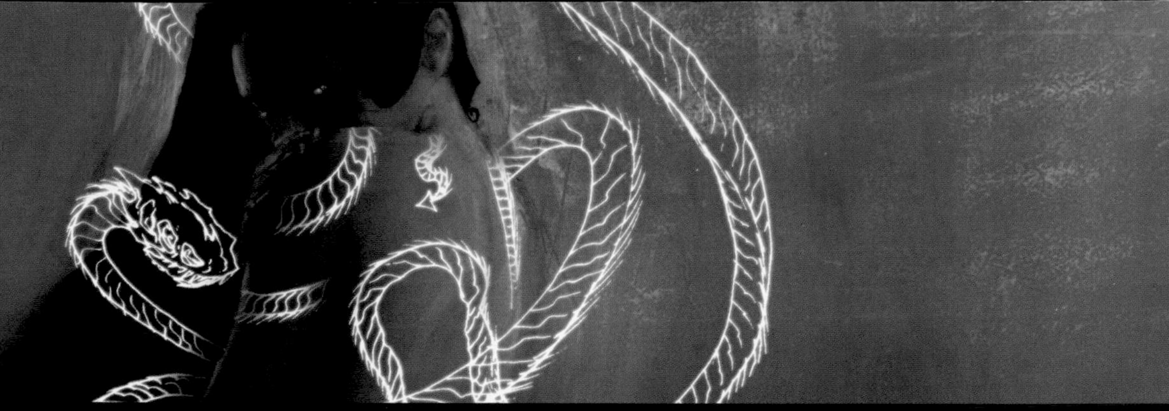

Tentacular Introductus

Great waving tentacular demons from the spaces between worlds.

Leprechauns imagined like angry, rutting, unfixed mongrel dogs.

Demonic skeletal strippers that hold back the gates of Hell in a local pub.

A homemade robot with the likeness of one half of ZZ Top, all presided over by a sentient worm that resides in the eye socket of a well-dressed corpse, and did I mention great big 'umongous fucking guns?

So to recap, tentacles-a-plenty, sex, guns, demons and beer. What more does one want for a 21st century graphic novel?

Welcome to the beautifully rendered and rather cheekily written *Wormwood Gentleman Corpse*, an idea that I happen to know has lingered in Ben Templesmith's imagination for decades, and here it emerges after great gestation from its pupae fitfully distilled, or perhaps sickeningly fermented into five paperbacks finally collected here in all their dripping viscera.

What makes Wormy such a charmer is a collision of things, a kind of auto wreck of irreverence:

Ben's down-to-Earth dialogue and settings make the world of Wormwood all too familiar, but the characters that inhabit it are clearly not. The man himself is cheerfully discourteous, with the voice of a pub-going bloke, surrounded by demons that speak in the same Earthly patter. It's a great schism, and I do love a bit of schism.

In keeping with the unpredictable, Wormwood has his head shot off within the first few following pages... what I like about this is not just that it comes from no-where but how the head is shot off:

It's with great splashes of ink, blur lines of orange, fire yellow flares with a backing of blood red specific to the marriage [illegible] writer/artist that just wouldn't work any other way. In fact, it is this marriage of a writer rendering with pencil, ink, paint and mouse spilling his deranged mind directly onto the page that, in my book, makes the gentleman corpse with his one wormy eye and his row of grinning rictus teeth fit to stride in the footprints of the many graphic novel character giants that have gone before him.

But enough gushing for now, first, a bit of history.

The *Book of Revelations*, as put out in the *New Testament* by John of Patmos, mentions Wormwood as a star that poisons all the waters of the earth and comes somewhat at the end of days.

Now John of Patmos was not the most reliable of Johns in the *Bible*, and if you care to look into the matter, you will find the *Bible* is full of Johns.

This John is not the one that scribbled down Gospels, nor John the Evangelist. In fact, this was John the (allegedly) hallucinogen-horking great nutter who liked to ramble on about giant great horse sized locust-scorpions with human heads and the teeth of lions that sting men without killing them for five months... nutter talk.

Some people have concluded that the Wormwood of the book of John is actually a prophecy fulfilled by Chernobyl, the Russian nuclear power station that went meltdown in the '80s, (Chernobyl translated in Ukrainian comes out as "Wormwood").

Then there is Artemisia absinthium, the plant called Wormwood from which that naughty drink Absinthe is made that is purported to have caused Kafka to write out of his box and Van Gogh to whip off his ear.

Somehow this all seems to fit and make sense to me despite the fact that young Mr. Ben Templesmith is one of the nicest, down-to-earth and most humble of human beings to possess such great reserves of artistry.

In fact, it's difficult at first to understand that he holds within him the propensity for such constructions of the apocalypse. Then you spend more time with him and see that dark glint in his eye, that flash of teeth in his smile and you become thankful that he is such a wonderfully maladjusted miscreant.

Behold *Wormwood Gentleman Corpse*. Harlan Ellison likes it and so do I...

DAVID SLADE
December 2006

Thanks to Arni, Mark and Wooller,

for the enthusiasm, opinions and alcohol.

Special thanks to

Douglas Adams, Terry Nation and Russell T. Davies

In memory of

Simon Temple

1982- 2006

Leroy's Special Brew

{ *The City* }

THE DARK ALLEY
SAD SEEDY LONERS WELCOME
THE DARK ALLEY
THE DARK ALLEY
THE DARK ALLEY
SAD SEEDY LONERS WELCOME
BOOMCHA
BOOMCHA
BOOMCHA
BOOMCHA
BOOMCHA
BOOMCHA
AAAAH, BEER.
BOOMCHA

THE DARK ELIXIR OF LIFE ITSELF.
NOTHING IS SO SWEET, SO MAJESTIC, SO--

--SO USELESS. YOU KNOW, ANYONE WITH HALF A BRAIN WOULD'VE ACTUALLY BUILT THEIR METALLIC CLOCKWORK COMPANION WITH AT LEAST SOME KIND OF ALCOHOL CONSUMPTION ABILITY IF HE'S MEANT TO BE A GLORIFIED DRINKING BUDDY.

MEH, MR PENDUL ME
I NEED TO ADJUST YOUR JOVIALITY COG WHEN WE GET HOME.

MEDUSA! FLEECING THE CUSTOMERS AS ALWAYS?
ENJOYING THE SHOW, BOYS?
I'VE GOT *NO BITS*.

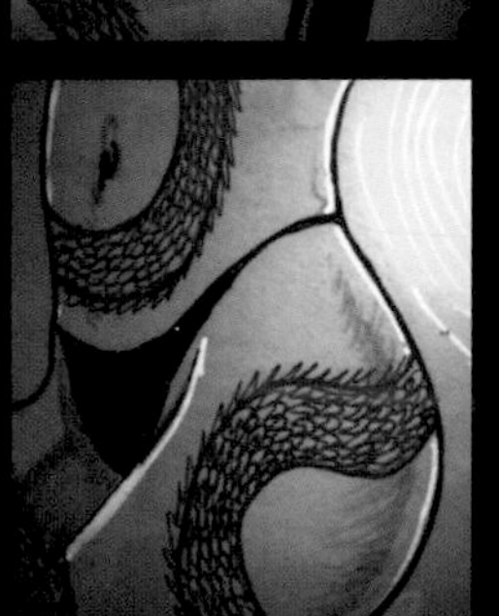

HEERRRRHHH...
ERM, QUITE LOVELY, YES.

SO IS, UH, PHOEBE ON ROSTER TONIGHT? I HAVE AN ERM... *JOB OFFER* FOR HER...
IS THAT WHAT THEY'R CALLING NOW?
NAH, WEDNESDAYS AND FRIDAYS. TUESDAYS IS CROSSBOW NIGHT.

YOU KNOW, I SHOULD HAVE GOTTEN A ZOMBIE SIDEKICK DRINKING BUDDY. THOSE GUYS DON'T BACKCHAT NEARLY AS MUCH.

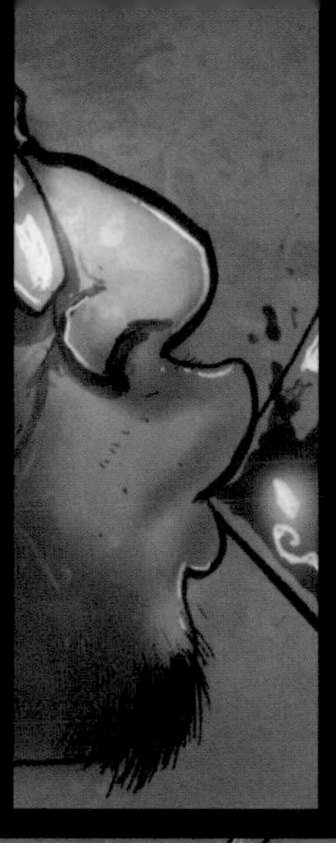

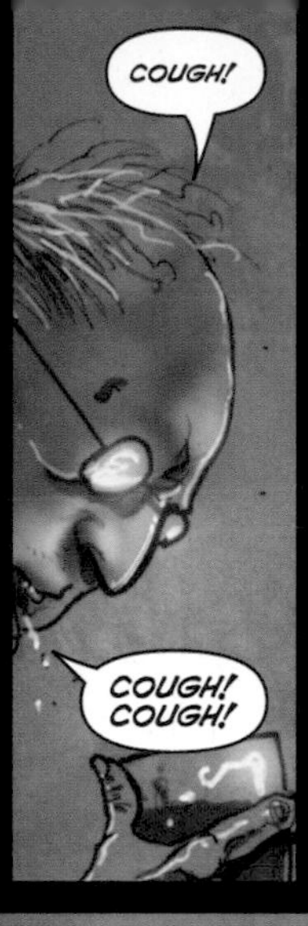
COUGH!
COUGH! COUGH!

HACK!

HURRK!

KKK--
KKKFFT--

INTERESTING.
DON'T SEE THAT SORT OF THING EVERY DAY.

THAT FLOWER?
KIND OF. MORE LIKE ... WEED ...OUGH.
I'M GOING TO LOSE CUSTOMERS... WELL, *MORE* CUSTOMERS... CAN'T YOU DO SOMETHING?

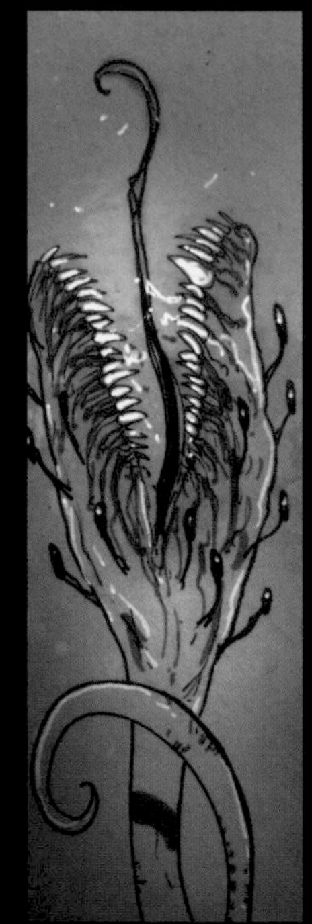

UHHH ...OU BROUGH... YOUR GUN, RIGHT?
YOU BET.

MIGHT ...ANT TO ...SE IT.

ANY TIME NOW WOULD BE GOOD, OLD CHAP.

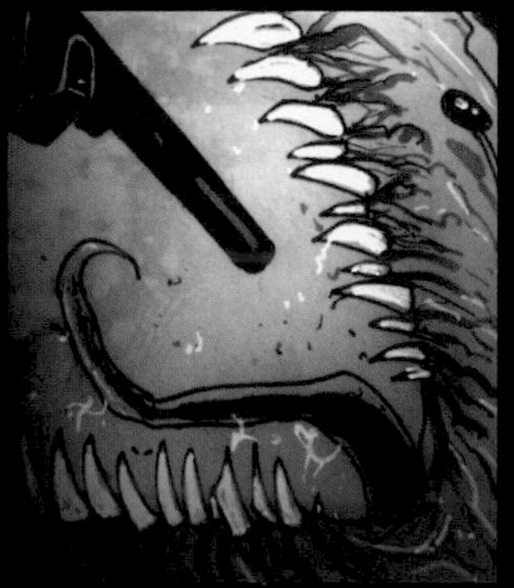

HEH.
TOOK YOUR TIME, MR. P.
MEDUSA, I THINK YOU MIGHT HAVE A PROBLEM HERE...

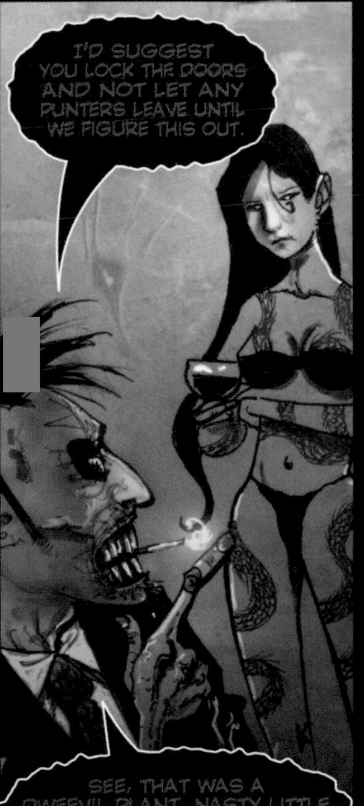
I'D SUGGEST YOU LOCK THE DOORS AND NOT LET ANY PUNTERS LEAVE UNTIL WE FIGURE THIS OUT.
SEE, THAT WAS A DWEEVIL PLANT. NASTY LITTLE THINGS, AND THERE'S PROBABLY GOING TO BE MORE OF THE LITTLE BUGGERS. HAVE A HABIT OF GROWING OUT OF HUMAN FLESH, THEY DO.

YOU HEARD THE CORPSE.
NOT UNTIL WE HAVE TO, DISCORDIA.
YES, MISS. HALF PRICE DANCES TO KEEP 'EM HAPPY?

OKAY. NEXT, WE NEED TO FIGURE OUT WHERE--
COUGH COUGH...

UH, OOOHHKK...

GHUURRRGGGHHH...
GHET GHIS GHING OGHGA GHEEE...
GHOOT, GHOOT, GHOOOOT GHAMN GHU!

ERM, YOU'RE SURE?
GHES, GHESSSS GHO IT!

GHUCKING GHELL, GHO IT!!!

WELL, OKAY. THIS'LL PROBABLY HURT A BIT.
GHUUURGH...

B-CHOOOM

AAAHHH, THAT'S THE TICKET.
OKAY, ANYONE GOT A STAPLER?

MINUTES AND 54 STAPLES LATER...
LOVELY.
CHEERS.
SO, WHAT THE HELL WAS THAT THING AND HOW DO WE GET RID OF THEM?

WELL, I'VE NOT SEEN DWEEVIL PLANTS AROUND HERE IN, OH, A GOOD THOUSAND YEARS, SO I'D SAY THEY CAME THROUGH THAT NIFTY DIMENSIONAL GATE YOU AND AND YOUR GIRLS ARE MEANT TO GUARD.
YEAH, THAT GATE.
PROBLEM IS, THERE'S BEEN MORE THAN ONE, SO I'D SAY WE'VE GOT A SPORE FATHER ON OUR HANDS.

LUCKILY, SINCE THIS IS THE FIRST BLOOM, HE SHOULD STILL BE RELATIVELY IMMATURE AND PRETTY EASY TO-
UHHH... NOT EXACTLY THE FIRST. WE'VE BEEN HAVING THESE THINGS POP UP THE BETTER HALF OF A WEEK NOW.
WE'VE PUT THEM ALL IN THE STOREROOM OVER THERE. HOPED YOU WOULDN'T NOTICE.

AAAAND YOU WERE GOING TO TELL ME ABOUT THIS WHEN EXACTLY??

SO, YOU THOUGHT YOU'D PUT THEM BACK HERE, HOPE NO ONE WOULD NOTICE THE SMELL OR THE FACT YOU'VE GOT A DOZEN OR SO MISSING STRIP CLUB PATRONS AND THEN WHAT?
WELL, UHHH...
THIS IS JUST *FANTASTIC*, INNIT? THIS MEANS THE SPORES COULD BE EVERYWHERE BY NOW. NOT ONLY THAT, THE SPORE FATHER WILL PROBABLY BE AT FULL MATURITY NOW. ONE TOUGH SONUVAFUNGUS.
YOU KNOW IT'S IN THE *CONTRACT FOR INTERDIMENSIONAL GATE STEWARDSHIP* THAT YOU'RE MEANT TO REPORT THIS STUFF.
IT'S THE LEAST YOU CAN DO IF YOU WANT TO KEEP THAT LITTLE *IMMORTALITY CLAUSE*, MEDUSA.
YEAH, YEAH, I KNOW! IT'S JUST THAT TIMES HAVE BEEN TOUGH LATELY. I COULDN'T AFFORD TO SHUT THE PLACE FOR A WEEK OR HOWEVER LONG IT'D TAKE JUST BECAUSE A FEW OF THE PUNTERS DIED. KNOW WHAT I MEAN?

SINCE *WHEN* HAS PROFIT BEEN A REASON TO PUT YOUR *ENTIRE* FUN LOVING, FLESH ENCRUSTED, BEER DRINKING, LAP DANCING DIMENSION AT RISK FROM THINGS THAT WILL EAT ALL THE MINDLESS PEONS HERE FROM THE INSIDE OUT AND *STILL* COMPLAIN ABOUT THE CALORIES, EH?

I THINK I MISS THE OLD MEDUSA. HONESTLY, DID YOU TURN INTO A COMPLETELY WHINEY LITTLE UNFUN *BITCH* ONCE WE STOPPED SHAGGING OR *WHAT?*

YOU SIGNED UP FOR THE GIG, GIRL. 1500 YEARS AGO OR SO. *IMMORTALITY IN EXCHANGE FOR LOOKING AFTER A DIMENSIONAL GATE.* PRETTY CUSHY JOB IF YOU ASK *ME.*

I MEAN, DO I HAVE TO GO TO THE *HIGH LORD OVERSEER'S OFFICE* AND GET HIM TO REVOKE YOUR LICENSE?

YES, I MISS THE OLD MEDUSA. THE ONE THAT'D RIP YOUR HEAD OFF, PISS DOWN THE NECK HOLE AS PART OF THE GOLDEN SHOWER SHOW AND PROCEED TO GIVE THE SPASMING CORPSE A 10 MINUTE LAPDANCE AND STILL EXPECT HIM TO TIP YOU.

AAAH, THOSE WERE THE DAYS.

[nostalgic moment]

THANKS, WORM. NOW I REMEMBER WHY I *DUMPED* YOU.
AH, YOU KNOW YOU STILL LOVE ME, BABY. AND BESIDES, YOU *ALWAYS* COME RUNNING BACK TO ME WHEN STUFF LIKE THIS GOES WRONG, NO?
BESIDES, YOU DON'T JUST GROW OUT OF A *NECROPHILIA* FETISH OVERNIGHT, DO YOU?
I CAN HANDLE THINGS MYSELF, JERKOFF.

ERR, MUCH AS I LOVE WATCHING THE *DOMESTICS*, WE HAVE A BUNCH OF CORPSES WITH *DEMON FUNGUS GROWING OUT OF THEM* AND SOME KIND OF *VEGETATIVE PATIENT ZERO REPRODUCING HIMSELF IN THE BAR'S ALCOHOL*.
SO WHAT'RE WE GOING TO *DO* ABOUT IT EXACTLY?

EASY.
INDUSTRIAL STRENGTH WEED KILLER.
WE SPRAY *EVERYTHING THAT MOVES* AND *HALF THE STUFF THAT DOESN'T.*
UM, WHAT ABOUT THE *HEALTH HAZARDS?* YOU CAN'T JUST SPRAY PEOPLE WITH STUFF LIKE THAT.
I KNOW A GUY, KILLED HIS MUM ONCE WHEN SHE TURNED OUT TO BE A SPIDER QUEEN FROM THE QUATH DIMENSION THAT EATS HER OFFSPRING ONCE THEY REACH 30. HE *OWES* ME.
YES, YES, BROKEN EGGS AND OMLETTES AND ALL THAT, I'M AFRAID. BIT LATE TO CARE *NOW*.

AND THEN I FIND THE SCUM WHO'S PUTTING HIS DEMON FILTH INTO ***MY*** *BEER.*

LOGIC DICTATES THAT IF ALL THE PEOPLE BEING USED AS SPORE HOSTS ARE DRINKERS, AS OPPOSED TO DANCERS, AND WE NARROW THAT DOWN TO THE FACT THAT ONLY PUNTERS DRINKING *BEER* SHOW SYMPTOMS... RIGHT?
RIGHT.
RIGHT, ONLY *BEER* DRINKERS ARE AFFECTED...
THEN I'D SAY WITHOUT A DOUBT, OUR CHAP WOULD BE THAT RATHER STRANGE LOOKING BARMAN TRYING TO LOOK INCONSPICOUS OVER THERE WHILE HE...

...OH.
...OH, THAT'S JUST GRAND.

YOU'VE BEEN STICKING YOUR WILLY IN THE LINES, HAVEN'T YOU? SICK DEVIANT.
NO... ERR... NO. ...OF COURSE NOT!

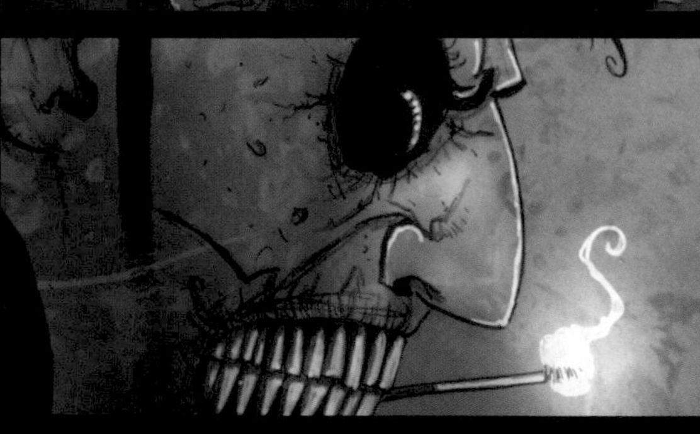
I THOUGHT I TASTED IT. DAMN IT, IT ALL MAKES SENSE NOW. WHAT EASIER WAY FOR A SPORE FATHER TO DO HIS WORK THAN SIMPLY JIZZING HIS SPORE INTO NOURISHING BEER BEFORE BEING TRANSFERRED TO HIS UNSUSPECTING HOSTS.

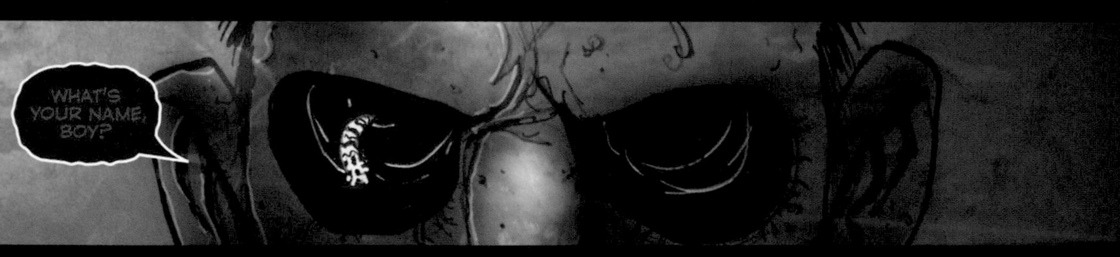
WHAT'S YOUR NAME, BOY?

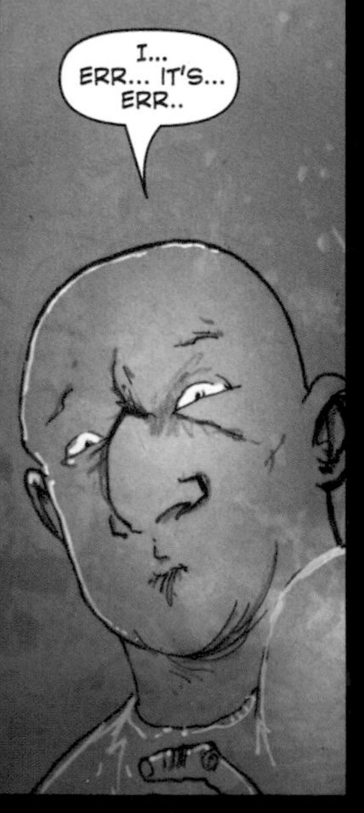
I... ERR... IT'S... ERR..

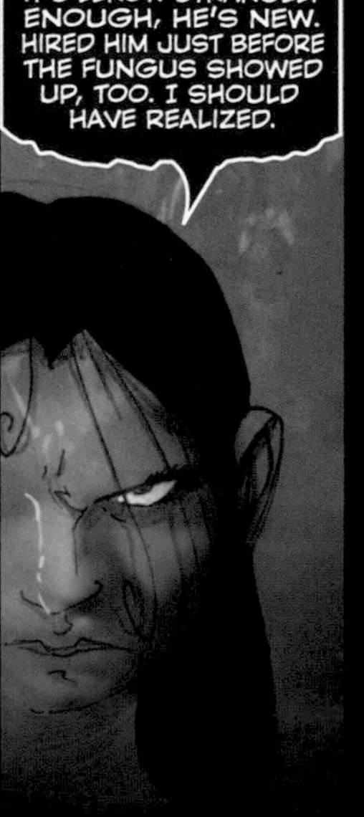
IT'S LEROY. STRANGELY ENOUGH, HE'S NEW. HIRED HIM JUST BEFORE THE FUNGUS SHOWED UP, TOO. I SHOULD HAVE REALIZED.

YOU NEVER WERE ONE TO CHECK REFERENCES, WERE YOU?
SHUT UP.

SO, LEROY...

I... I DON'T KNOW WHY I DID IT... IT JUST, YOU KNOW... FELT SO GOOD...

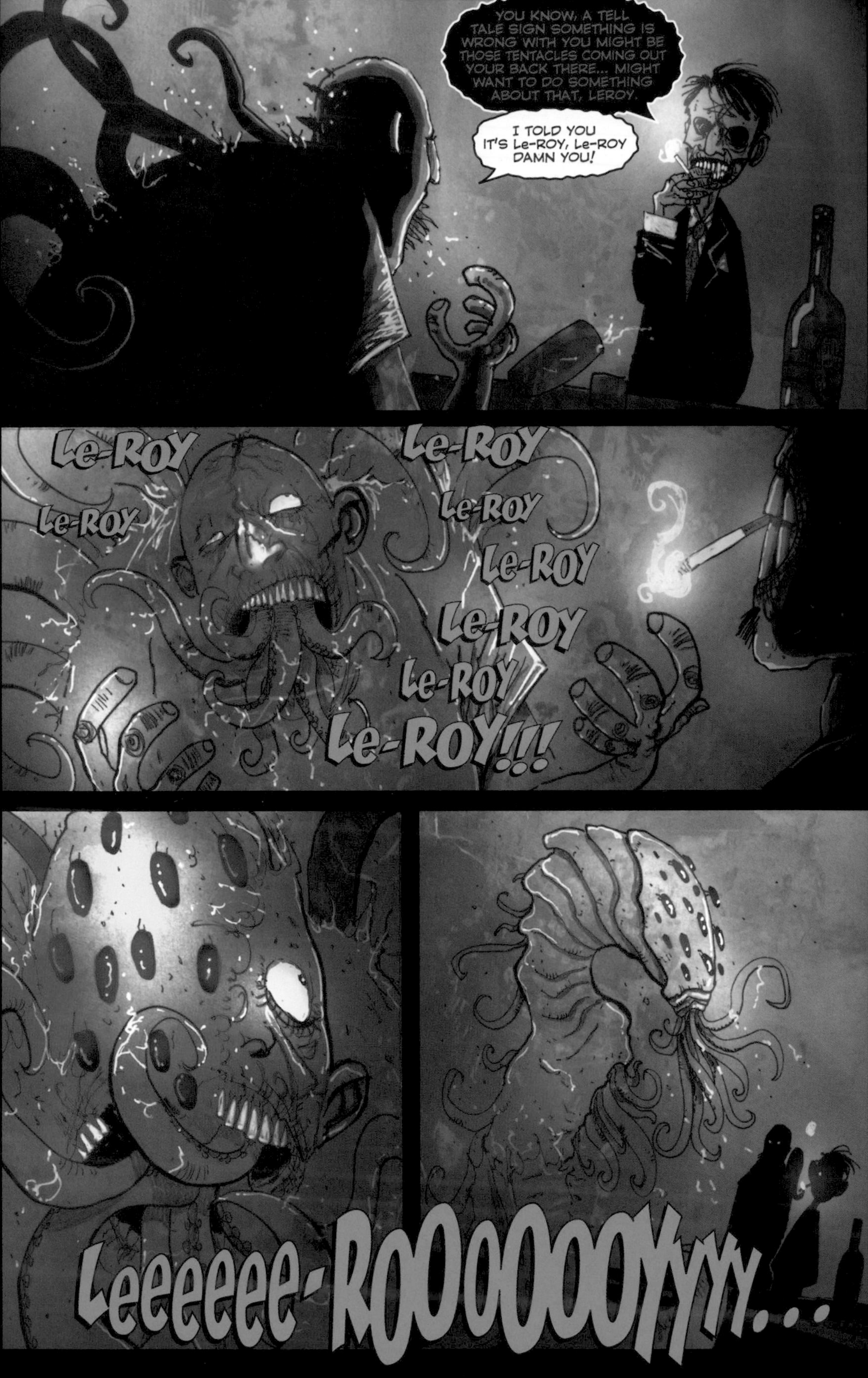

YOU KNOW, A TELL TALE SIGN SOMETHING IS WRONG WITH YOU MIGHT BE THOSE TENTACLES COMING OUT YOUR BACK THERE... MIGHT WANT TO DO SOMETHING ABOUT THAT, LEROY.

I TOLD YOU IT'S Le-ROY, Le-ROY DAMN YOU!

Le-ROY

Le-ROY

Le-ROY

Le-ROY

Le-ROY

Le-ROY

Le-ROY

Le-ROY!!!

Leeeeee-ROOOOOOYYYY...

WELL, THERE YOU GO. JUST MADE A WHOLE LOT MORE TROUBLE FOR US, DIDN'T YOU, MR. MOTOR MOUTH.
QUIET, PENDULUM. IT WAS IMPORTANT TO DRAW THE TRUE SPORE FATHER OUT OF THE HOST. ONLY WAY TO DO THAT WAS THROUGH ANGER.
AND NOW WE KILL IT.
HAVE I TOLD YOU HOW SICK I AM OF TENTACLES?
MANY TIMES. REMIND ME TO REMOVE THE "MR. P WHINEY BITCH CIRCUIT" LATER, WOULD YOU?

HERE WE GO AGAIN, THEN.
OH, CHEER UP. REMEMBER QINGU, THAT RECTAL PROBING BATTLE COMMANDER OF TIAMET? NASTY BUGGER. THIS COULD BE SO MUCH WORSE.
THANKS FOR REMINDING ME. MY COGS DIDN'T NEED LUBRICATING FOR A FULL 6 MONTHS THANKS TO THAT GUY. STILL TRYING TO WASH HIS STINK OFF.

YOU ARE SO FIRED.

MEDUSA, OPEN THAT BLOODY PORTAL OF YOURS, WILL YOU? THIS THING IS GETTING... PERSONAL.

ERK!

INTER DIMENSIONAL CELL PHONE (EASY MINUTES PLAN)
CALLING

EDNA? HI. YEAH.

YEAH. GOOD THANKS, YEAH. HOW'RE THE KIDS?

MEDUSA!

ALRIGHT, ALRIGHT...YEAH, SORRY, EDNA. CAN YOU? THANKS. OWE YOU ONE. TA.
NOW.
PISS OFF.

LOOK AT MY CLUB. HAPPY?
VERY.
BLINK

SO WHAT NOW?

NOW?

AH, THANK YOU, CHLOE.

NOW, TWO SIPS OF THIS FOR EVERYONE STILL ALIVE, AND CALL ME IN A COUPLE WEEKS. FIX ANYONE STILL INFESTED RIGHT UP, IT WILL. TRUST ME.
AGENT ORANGE

Birds, Bees, Blood & Beer

Chapter 1

HMM...
CanceR
Sticks
ahoy!

SO, YOU'RE LIKE WHAT, A MONSTER HUNTER OR SOMETHING?
OH GOD, NO. ONLY A MORON WOULD ACTUALLY GO LOOKING FOR THE BLOODY THINGS. I JUST TEND TO, UH... ATTRACT A CERTAIN TYPE OF PEOPLE. YES, THAT'S IT.
AND BY "PEOPLE," YOU MEAN LARGE MAN-EATING, TENTACLED THINGS AND STUFF?
WELL, YEAH, BUT YOU SAY THAT LIKE IT'S A BAD THING. SOME OF THEM CAN BE RATHER LOVELY CHAPS, YOU KNOW.

YEAH, I'M SURE. THAT'S WHY YOU'RE WANTING ME TO BE SOME KIND OF PSEUDO BODYGUARD EYE-CANDY, RIGHT? BECAUSE THEY'RE ALL SUCH "LOVELY CHAPS."
I SAID SOME, NOT ALL. ANYWAYS, YOU WOULDN'T HAVE TO DEAL WITH THEM OFTEN. MOSTLY, YOU'D BE BACKING UP MR. PENDULUM HERE.
HEYA.
PENDULUM IS MY DRINKING PAL AND ERR... SHOTGUN ENTHUSIAST. HE'S A HARDY FELLOW, BUT NOT SO BIG ON THE CONVERSATION, IF YOU KNOW WHAT I MEAN.
BESIDES WHICH, SOMEONE WITH YOUR TALENTS WOULD COME IN QUITE USEFUL.
YOU REALIZE I MAKE GOOD MONEY HERE, RIGHT? WHY WOULD I WANT TO SPEND MY TIME BABYSITTING A CORPSE-POSSESSING SENTIENT MAGGOT AND HIS FRIEND, WHO'S APPARENTLY MADE OUT OF A FEW HUNDRED BEER CANS?

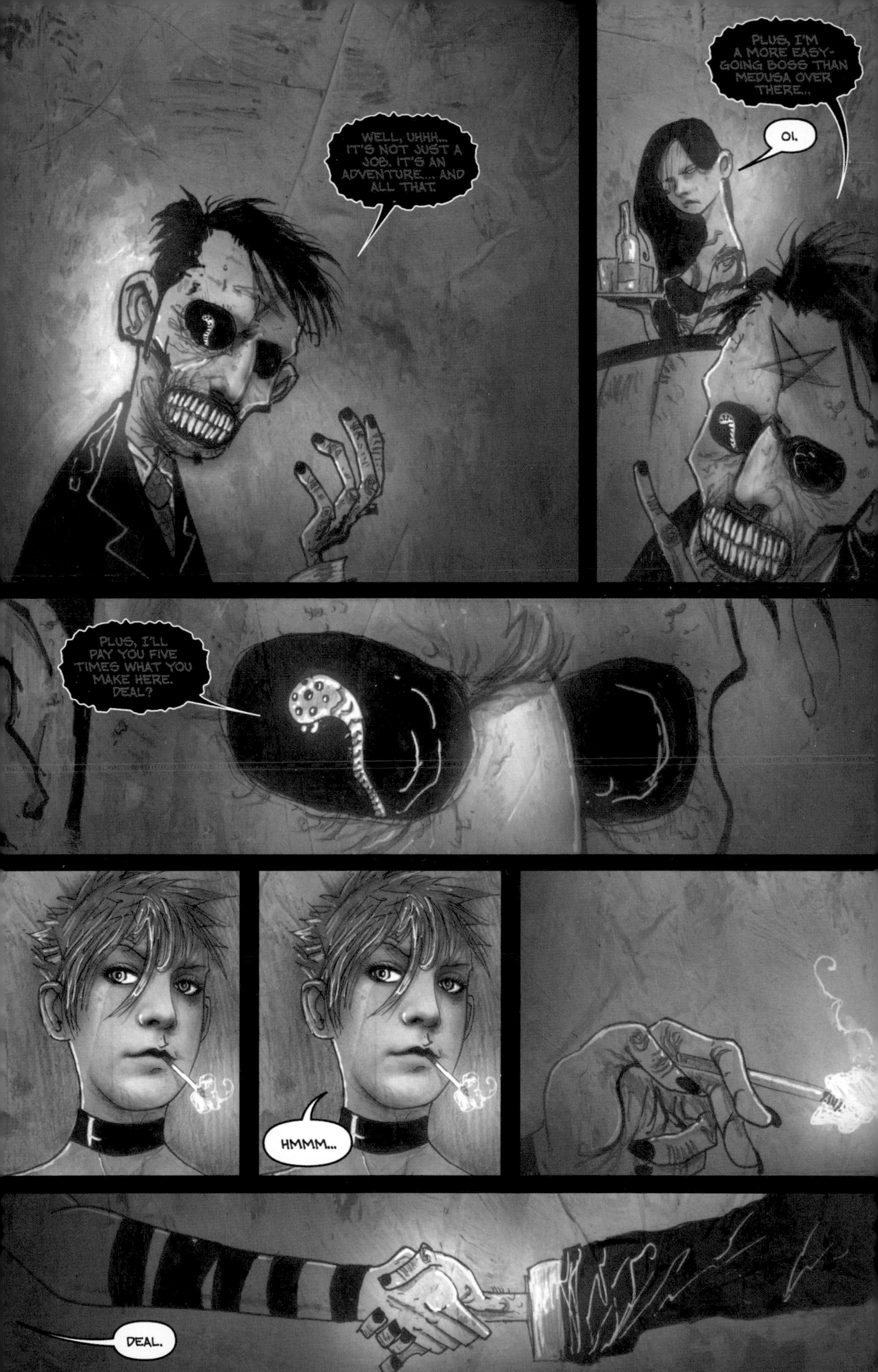
WELL, UHHH... IT'S NOT JUST A JOB, IT'S AN ADVENTURE... AND ALL THAT.
PLUS, I'M A MORE EASY-GOING BOSS THAN MEDUSA OVER THERE...
OI.
PLUS, I'LL PAY YOU FIVE TIMES WHAT YOU MAKE HERE. DEAL?
HMMM...
DEAL.

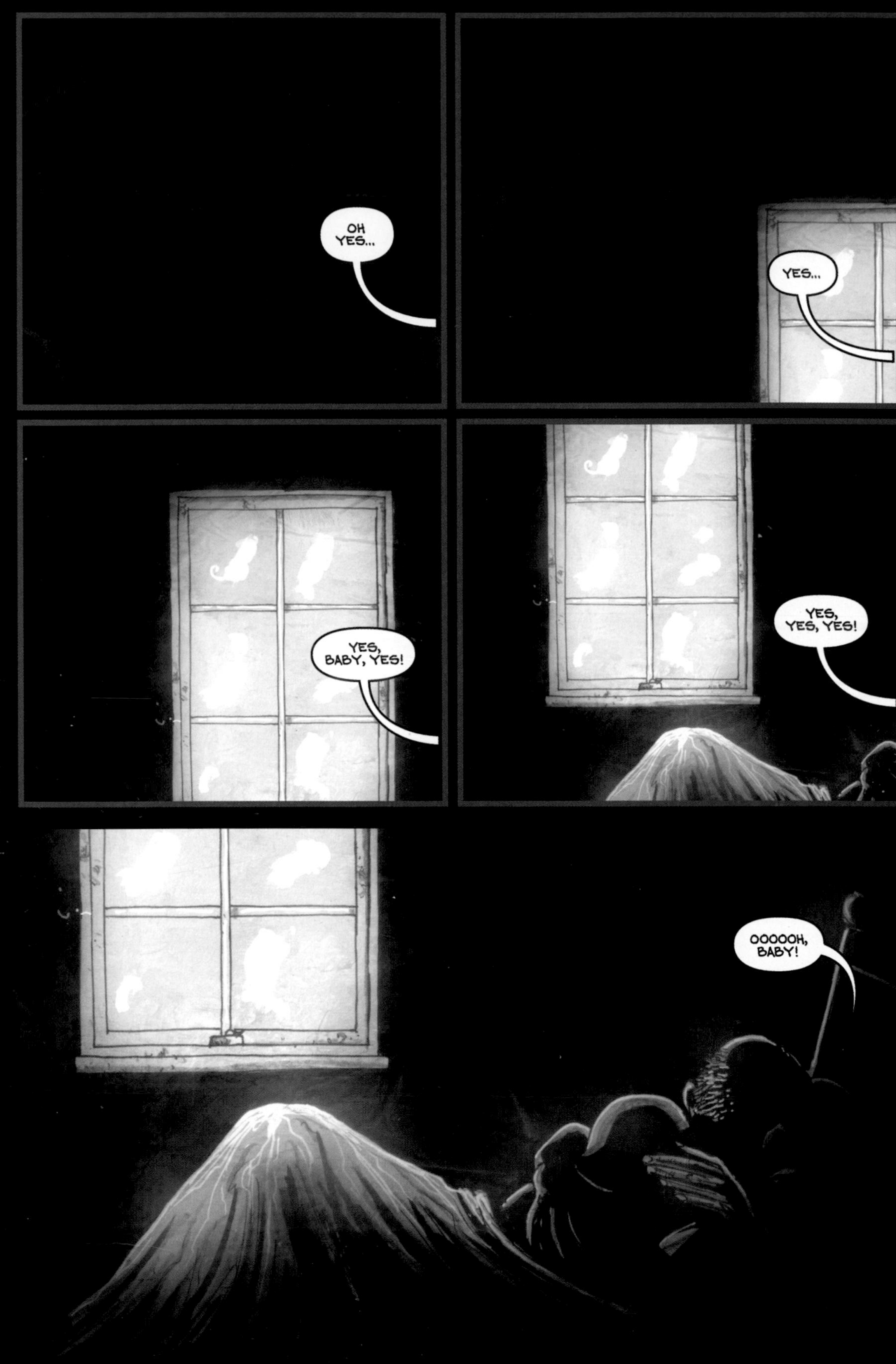
OH YES...
YES...
YES, BABY, YES!
YES, YES, YES!
OOOOOH, BABY!

OH, GEORGE, I DON'T KNOW WHAT'S DIFFERENT ABOUT YOU, BUT I LIKE IT.
WELL, NOW THAT YOU MENTION IT, I—WHAT WAS THAT?
I... I DON'T KNOW... MAYBE THOSE BEANS I HAD? IT... IT HURTS A BIT...
BLURK
JESUS, WHAT THE—
BLURRRRKK
AAAAAH!
MAKE IT STOP!
RRRRRKKKK
GOD, MAKE IT STOP!

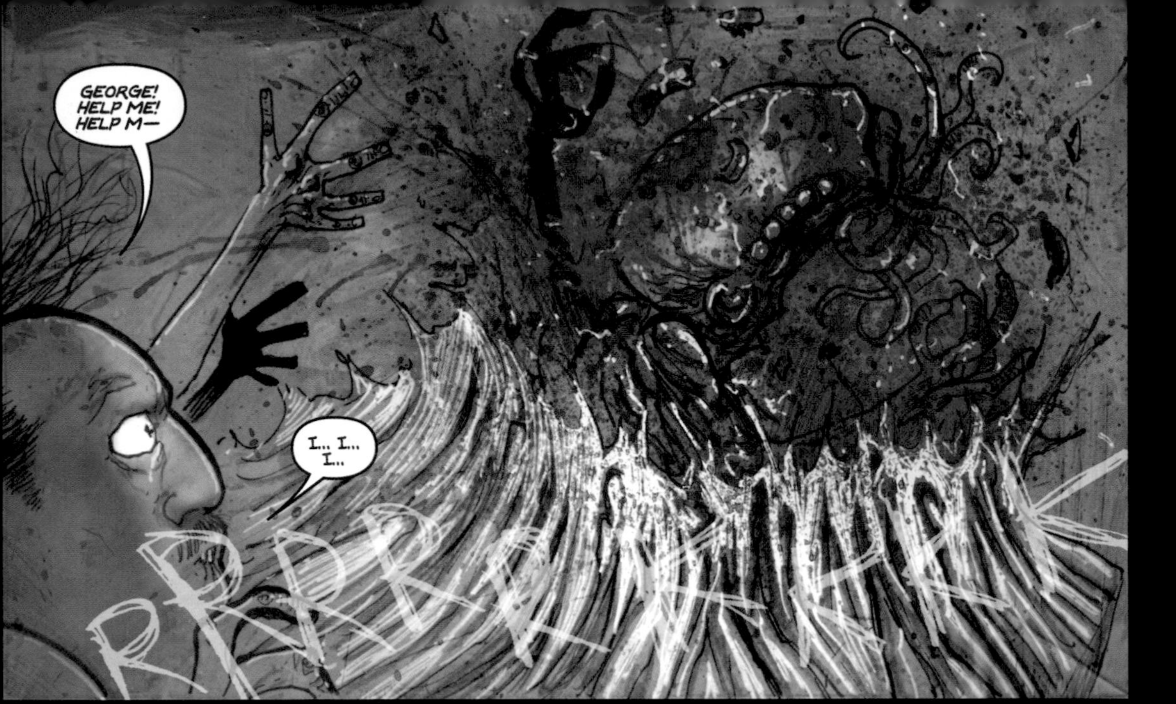

GEORGE! HELP ME! HELP M—

I... I... I...

I... I... PLEASE... I...
SSSHHLLKK

(TWITCH)
(TWITCH)

KKSSSSSHHHH

ALL THIS IS YOURS?

WELL, NO. I HAVE ESTATES IN EUROPE AND THE ELSEWHERE, TOO. THIS IS JUST MY FAVORITE RIGHT NOW.

THIS IS MY STUDY.
THIS IS MY SPECIMEN ROOM. I ALSO BREW BEER HERE. DON'T EVER CONFUSE THE TWO. I HAVE.

AND THIS IS MY ARMORY.

NICE. HOW EXACTLY DO YOU PAY FOR ALL THIS?

PATENTS. LET'S JUST SAY, EVERY TIME YOU SIT DOWN TO TAKE A CRAP.. SOME OF IT FLOATS MY WAY.

OKAAAAY...

DON'T LOOK AT ME. CAN'T USE A TOILET. GOT NO BITS.

WORMY, YOU HERE?

CHRIST... TROTSKY... I KNOW YOU'RE DEAD BUT THERE IS SUCH THING AS A DOOR.
YEAH, YEAH, SORRY ABOUT THAT... OOOOH, WHO'S THE LADY?
PHOEBE, NEW PERSONAL ASSISTANT... TROTSKY, LAZY DEAD GHOST COP.
LAZY?

WELL, YOU'RE MEANT TO BE WORKING OFF YOUR KARMIC DEBT SO YOU CAN MOVE ON. YET I SEEM TO BE THE ONE SOLVING ALL OF YOUR CASES, DON'T I?
WELL, I, ERR...

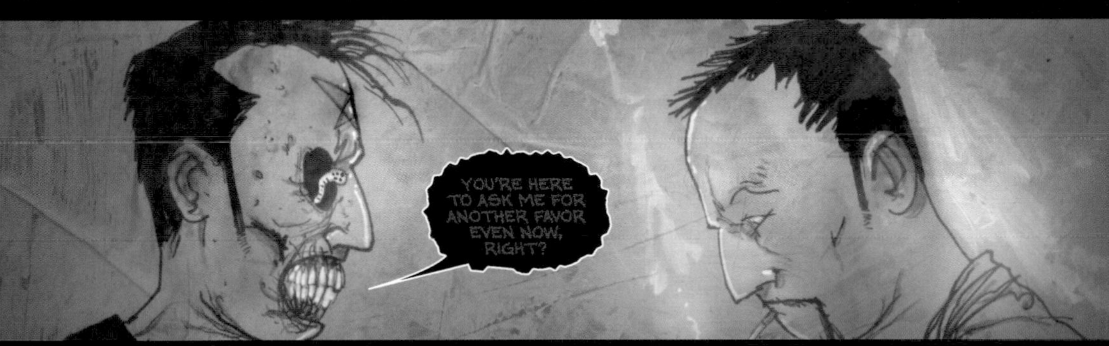
YOU'RE HERE TO ASK ME FOR ANOTHER FAVOR EVEN NOW, RIGHT?

MAAAAAYBE...

SIGH. SO WHAT IS IT THIS TIME?

GOT A SPATE OF RATHER VIOLENT BIRTHS RESULTING IN EXTREME CASES OF, UH, DEATH... WITH THE BABIES NOWHERE TO BE FOUND.

SOUNDS LIKE THAT CELEBRITY CASE YOU HAD ME COME IN ON LAST MONTH...
NO, THESE ARE DIFFERENT. THESE ONES WERE ALIVE DURING THE BIRTH AND SEEMED TO COME OUT OF THE USUAL PLACE, NOT THE HEAD. I—
YOU BASTARD! YOU MUST PAY!
CCRaaaSHH

I'M SORRY, WHAT?
I'LL KILL YOU!

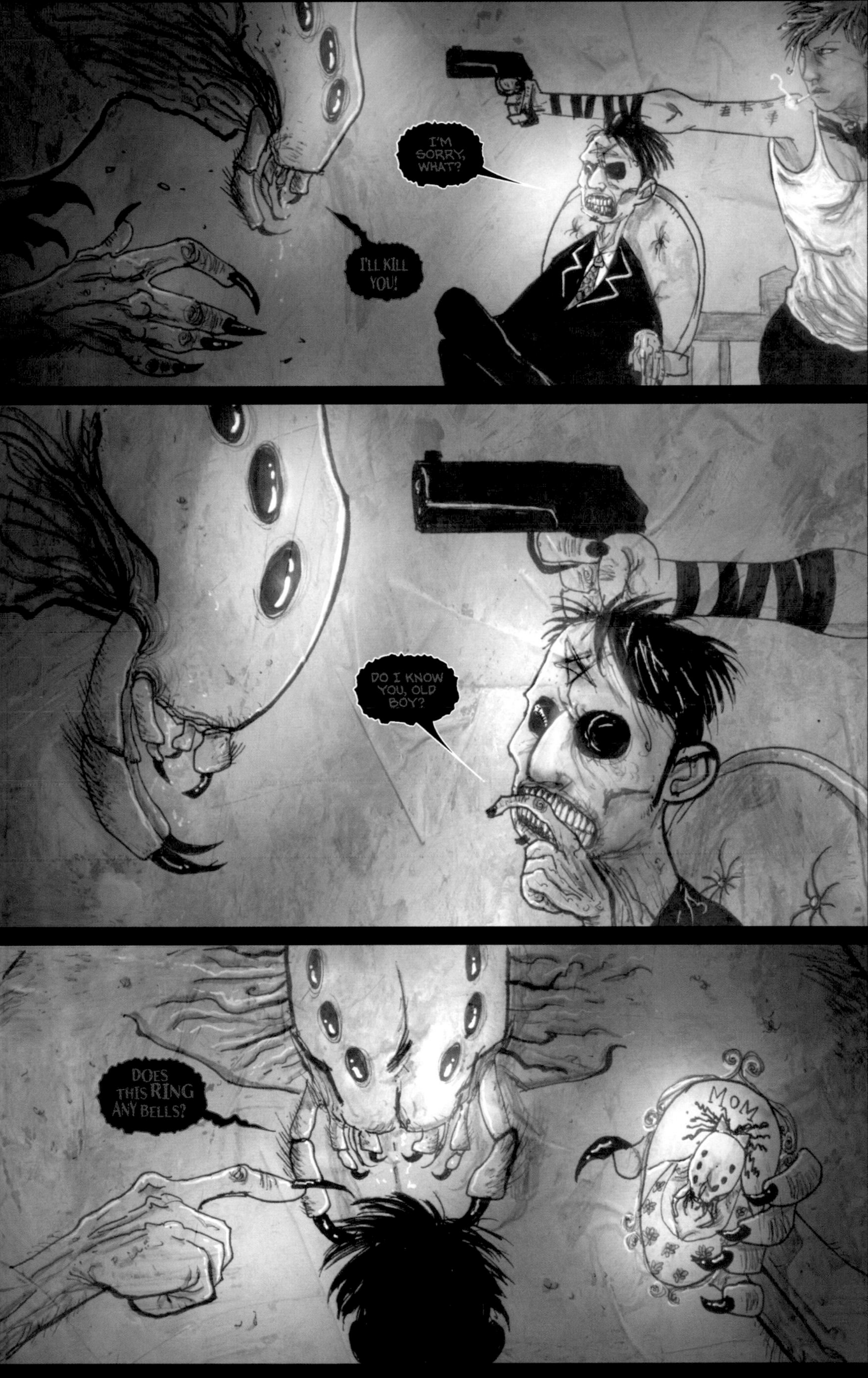

DO I KNOW YOU, OLD BOY?

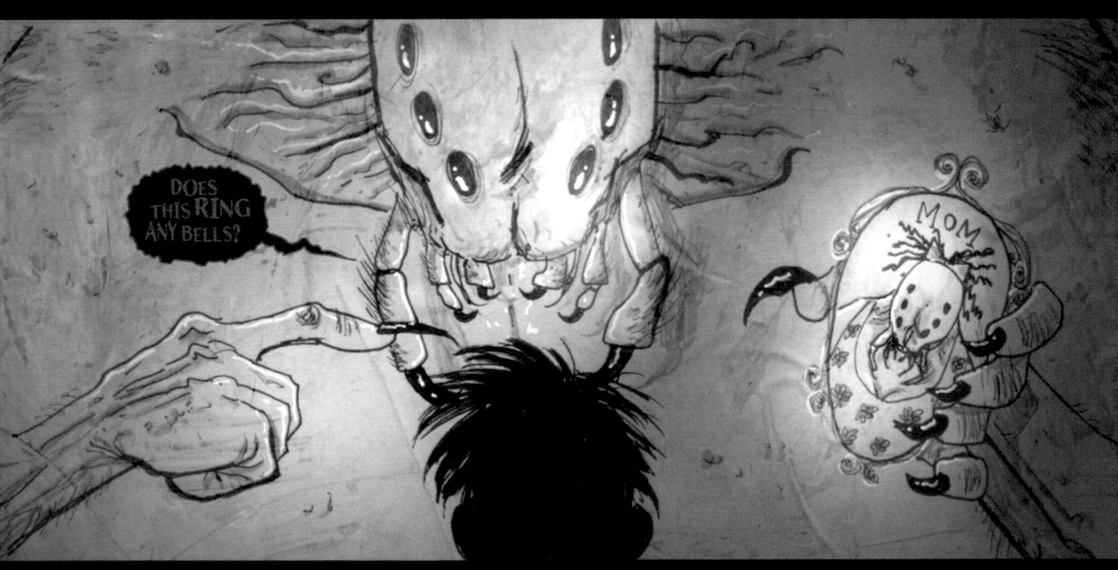
DOES THIS RING ANY BELLS?
MOM

OOOOOOH...
YOU MUST BE MUMMY'S BOY. LOOK, THIS IS ALL A BIT OF A MISUNDERSTANDING. I DIDN'T EXACTLY SLEEP WITH HER. IN FACT, SHE WANTED TO INSEMINATE MY BRAIN FULL OF HER EGGS AND—
I KNOW.
OH, I SEE...
BE SEEING YOU THEN.
BOOM
BOOM

YEAH,
BLAM
BLAM BLAM
BLAM BLAM
BLAM etc...
BAM
BYE,

YOU REALIZE I HAVEN'T EVEN SIGNED A CONTRACT YET, RIGHT?
SIGH.
BLAM
BLAM
BLAM

BLAM
BLAM
BLAM
BLAM
BLAM
BLAM
BLAM BLAM
BLAM BLAM
BLAM etc...
CLICK
CLICK
CLICK

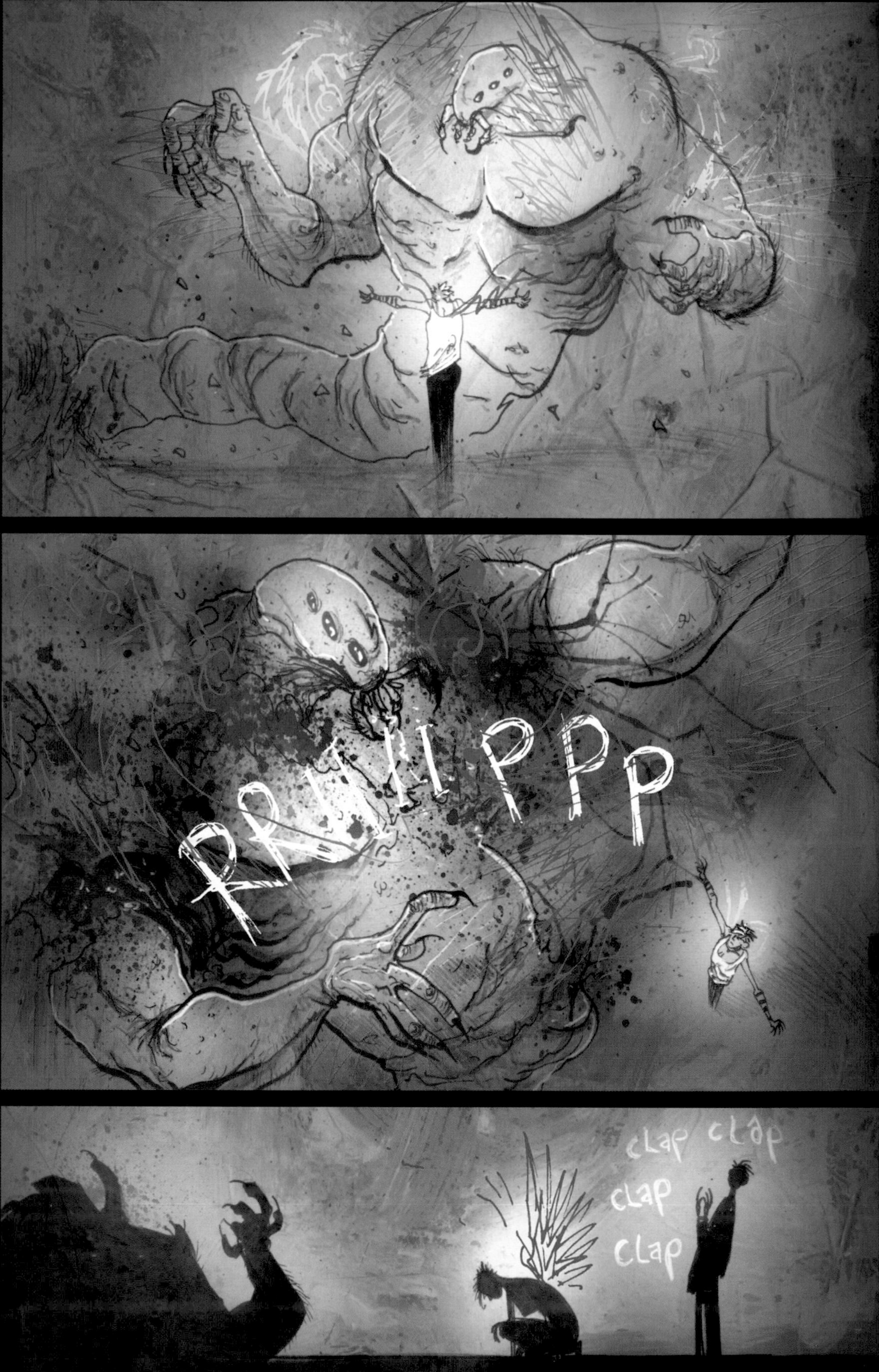
RRIIIPPP
clap clap
clap
clap

LOVELY. YOUR LITTLE GIFT FROM THE SISTERHOOD, I ASSUME? THE CLEANERS WILL BE HERE FOR A WEEK.
YOU'RE WELCOME.
ALRIGHTY, TROTSKY...
TELL ME ABOUT THESE EXPLODING WOMBS.

Chapter 2

Fatso's
GYM

PSST...

PSSSSST...

HUH?
YOU TALKING
TO ME?

YOU NICE AND SWEATY? YOU LIKE TO WORK OUT, EH? LIKE TO LOOK GOOD FOR THE LADIES, EH?
BIT TIRED? BIT TIRED AND OLD, BUT WISH YOU WERE YOUNGER, EH?
LOOKING FOR A LITTLE PICK-ME-UP? EH? EEEH?
WELL, UH, NO, I...
SURE YOU ARE... SURE YOU ARE. WANT TO BE A HIT WITH THE LADIES, A HIT, EH?
WANT A LITTLE SOMETHING TO ASSIST WITH THE OLD IN-OUT IN-OUT, EH?

UMMM...

BET A MAN LIKE YOU—FINE MAN LIKE YOU—HAS NO TROUBLE WITH THE LADIES, EH? BUT ALWAYS LOOKING TO MAKE THOSE MOMENTS JUST A LITTLE MORE MEMORABLE, EH? A LITTLE BIGGER, EH? WHAT DO YOU SAY, EH?

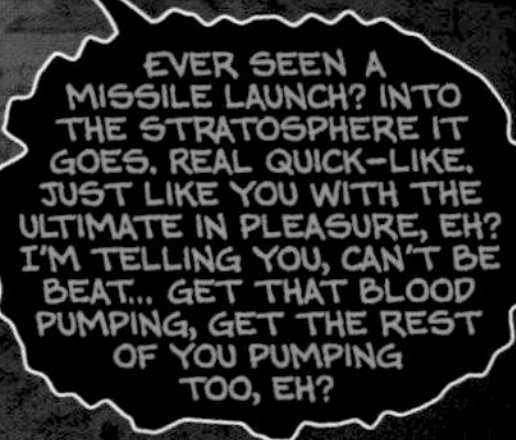

DARK ALLEY
SAD SEEDY LONERS WELCOME

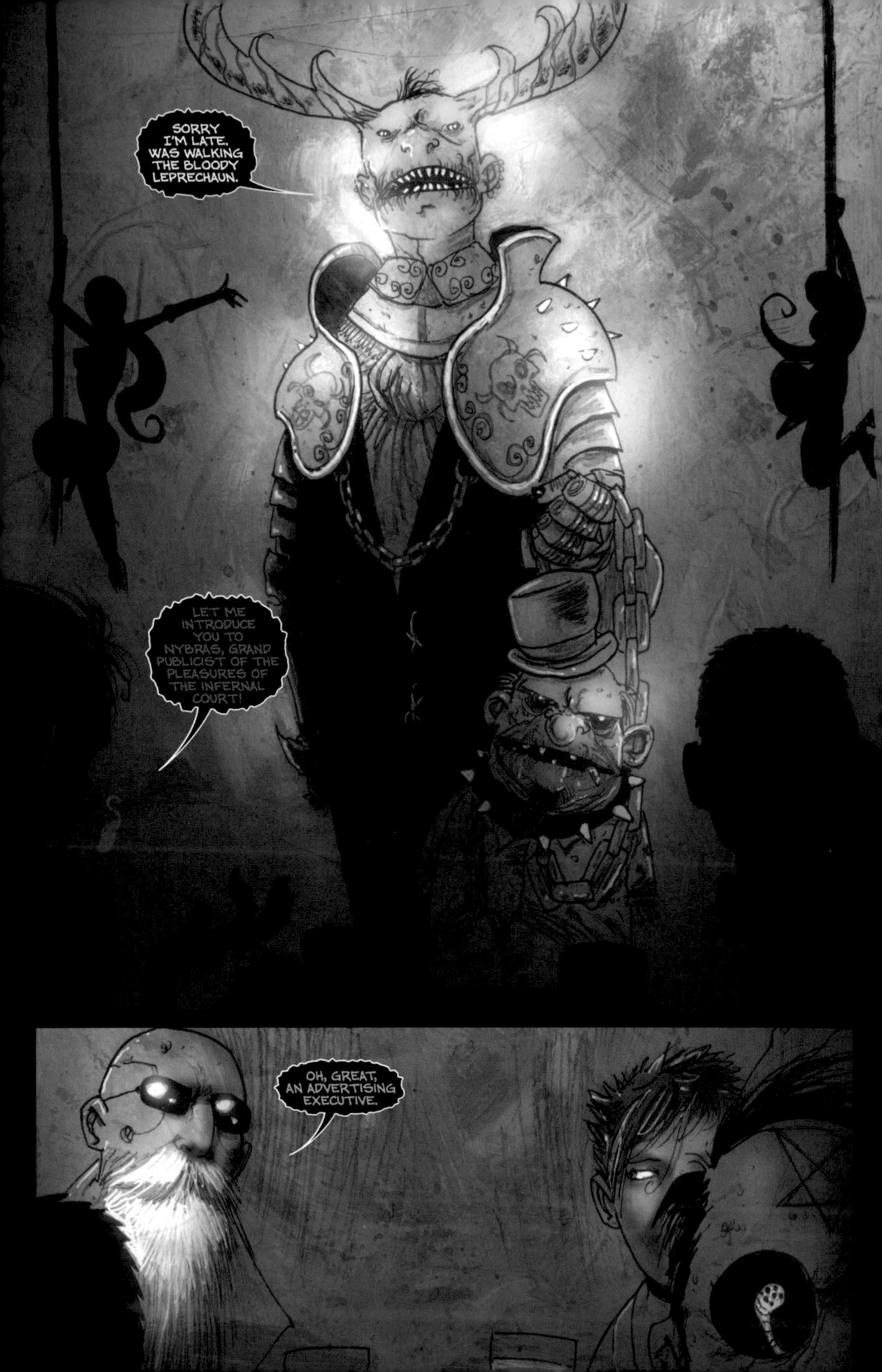
SORRY I'M LATE. WAS WALKING THE BLOODY LEPRECHAUN.
LET ME INTRODUCE YOU TO NYBRAS, GRAND PUBLICIST OF THE PLEASURES OF THE INFERNAL COURT!
OH, GREAT, AN ADVERTISING EXECUTIVE.

LONG TIME, NO SEE, WORM. NEW CORPSE? STILL INDULGING YOURSELF IN THE PLEASURES THIS REALM IS FAMOUS FOR, I SEE.
ALCOHOL AND COMFY FURNITURE.
BUT OF COURSE. YOU STILL HAVE THAT TIMESHARE HERE, DON'T YOU?
YES, YES... THE LARVAE AND I SHOULD BE USING IT IN A COUPLE MONTHS. YOU'LL HAVE TO COME UP FOR A VISIT SOMETIME.
AARRR... YBRRR ARMMMGAR RADISHRRR GLUMBRR B'KRAHRR NUB. RUMPA PUMPA!
PLK
I'M SORRY?
TBEESHRRR TBESHRRRR!
STOP THAT.

WHAT'S THAT STENCH? LIKE... ROTTING LAWN CLIPPINGS?
PLK

Blarrrfff
WHA-

CALM DOWN MR. P, IT'S JUST A LEPRECHAUN. THAT OVERPOWERING STENCH OF CLOVER... HE'S IN HEAT.

POOR BUGGER APPEARS TO BE HORNY AS HELL FOR YOU. THROWING HIS BEER IS A SIGN OF AFFECTION WHERE HE'S FROM. HE'S MARKED YOU AS HIS BITCH. MAYBE, IF YOU'RE LUCKY HE'LL SHOW YOU HIS LITTLE "POT OF GOLD."

Scratch Scratch

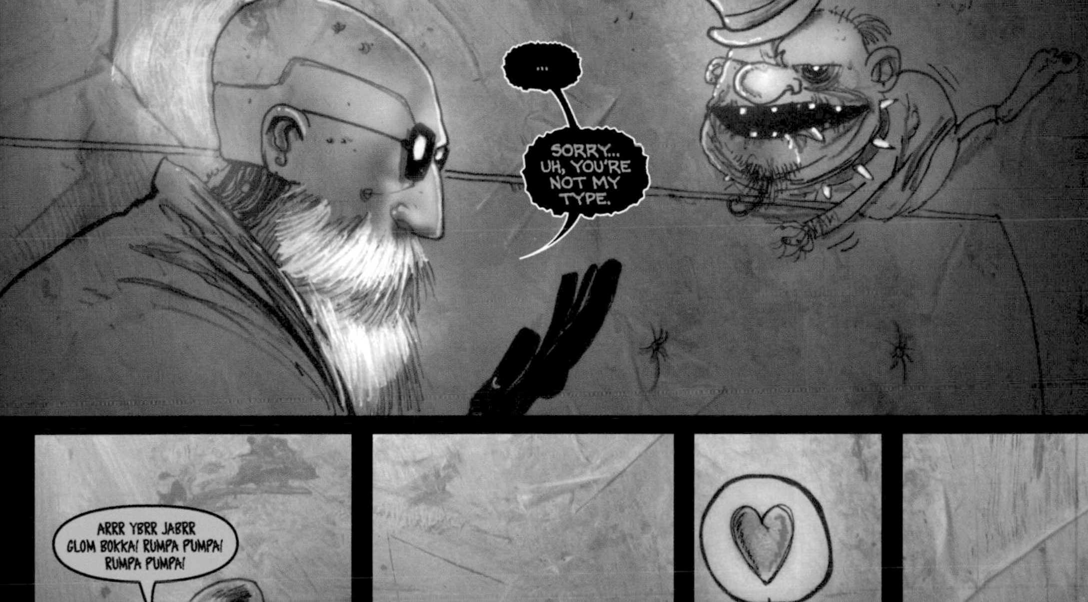

BOOM

GREAT. THAT'LL SET BACK LEPRECHAUNI RELATIONS CENTURIES, THAT WILL.
IT WAS MY WIFE'S.
I TRUST YOUR BOY WILL BE REIMBURSING ME. IT WAS A PEDIGREE, YOU KNOW.
I'LL TAKE CARE OF IT, DON'T WORRY, OLD CHAP.

SO, ANYWAY, YOU REALLY HAVEN'T HEARD ANYTHING AROUND THE PLACE? NONE OF YOUR OLD EMPLOYERS DOING ANYTHING OUT OF THE ORDINARY LATELY?
NAH. HONESTLY, MOST OF THEM ARE RETIRED.
MORE INTERESTED IN GARDENING AND INCONTINENCE PADS THESE DAYS, IF YOU ASK ME.

WORMY, THERE'S BEEN ANOTHER ONE. CRIME SCENE IS STILL, UH, FRESH.
EXCELLENT!

WELL, THANKS, NYBRAS, IT'S BEEN FUN BUT I MUST DASH. FEEL FREE TO PUT WHATEVER YOU WANT ON MY TAB. MEDUSA WILL TAKE CARE OF YOU. TAKE CARE, EH?
DITTO. AND DON'T FORGET, WE SIMPLY MUST DO A PROPER DINNER SOMETIME.
COUNT ON IT.

A SHORT TIME EARLIER...
WHUPP
OH, YES...
YESSS...
WHUPP
HARDER...
WHUPP
YOU'VE BEEN A VERY, VERY NAUGHTY BOY, MR. ASHCROFT...
OOOH, MAKE ME CRY... MAKE ME BEG!
I CAN DO BETTER THAN THAT BABY. I CAN MAKE YOU SCREAM...
naughty boy
OH, YES! OH, YE-URRRKKK

ERRK-
TOFU
HELP... ME...
JESUS!
SWEETIE, I'VE HAD PLENTY OF CLIENTS WORSE THAN YOU...

ZZZZZZZZZZZZZZZZZZZZZZZZ
WHUCK
(OUCH)

AND WHO MIGHT YOU BE, SIR?
HELLO
WHY, ISN'T IT OBVIOUS, OFFICER?
AND DON'T WORRY. THEY'RE WITH ME.

MY APOLOGIES DETECTIVE— JUST DIDN'T RECOGNIZE YOU.
OK, I'LL BITE... HOW IS IT EVERYONE WE MEET SEEMS TO HAVE NO PROBLEM WITH YOU BEING A ROTTING CORPSE WITH A WORM SPEAKING OUT OF AN EYE SOCKET?
POLICE
OH, JUST A LITTLE ENCHANTMENT I ALWAYS PUT ON WHEN I LEAVE THE HOUSE—UNLESS I'M IN L.A. PEOPLE JUST SEE WHAT THEY WANT TO SEE REALLY.
EXCEPT THE GIFTED ONES, OF COURSE. PEOPLE LIKE YOU ARE A LITTLE HARDER TO BULLSHIT.
OH, NOW THIS IS LOVELY. JUST LOVELY. DO WE ACTUALLY HAVE A BODY, OR DID A SLUSHY MACHINE JUST HAVE AN ORGASM?

BODIES, SIR. ONE OVER THERE... CHAINED UP.. THE OTHER IS OVER THERE. AND ERR, THERE... AND THERE... AND... THERE...
HMMM... BIT OF A DRAMA QUEEN, I THINK SHE WAS. OBVIOUSLY DIDN'T GO QUIETLY.
YOU COULD SAY THAT. I THINK SHE WAS MY KIND OF WOMAN.
SO ANOTHER BURSTER, I SEE, TROTSKY..
RIGHT. BU PERHAPS IT MORE TO DO WITH THE SEX INVOLVED... OR LACK OF, AS THE CASE MAY BE. THIS GUY WAS JUST BEING, UH, WHIPPED BY MISTRESS KOULTIER, SO FAR AS I CAN TELL.
AND IT APPEARS IT DOESN'T REALLY MATTER WHO OR WHAT GESTATES THEM. THIS IS THE FIRST MALE VICTIM, RIGHT?
YOU KNEW HER NAME? BEEN HERE BEFORE, EH, TROTSKY?
UMM... A CONVERSATIO FOR ANOTHER TIME..
OOOH, WHAT'S THIS? ONE OF THESE THINGS IS NOT LIKE THE OTHER. HMMM...
WHAT ABOUT THESE?
MOST INTERESTING. WE'LL TAKE THOSE, TOO.
ALRIGHT, I'M OFF TO SEE A MAN ABOUT A LEG.

NYSROGH'S TASTEY MEATS!

HEY, NYSROGH, YOU STILL OPEN?

BUT OF COURSE. FOR YOU, I'M ALWAYS OPEN. PROVIDED, OF COURSE, YOU'RE HERE TO BUY SOMETHING.

HOW MUCH WILL A LITTLE INFO COST ME TODAY THEN, NYS?
WELL, I GOT IN OME LOVELY RUMP F DRYAD TODAY. BUT STLY, I THINK YOU CAN'T GO PAST A COUPLE CYCLOPEAN TESTICLES. QUITE A COUP THAT WAS, CONSIDERING HOW RARE THEY ARE. I MEAN IT'S NOT LIKE THE THINGS HAVE TWO OF THEM TO COLLECT EACH TIME YOU MANAGE TO HUNT ONE OF THE BASTARDS DOWN, NOW, IS IT?
UHHH... OKAY, CYCLOPEAN BALL IT IS.
YOU WON'T BE PPOINTED. MAKES N EXCELLENT MORNAY SAUCE, I THINK YOU'LL FIND.
SHLLPK
THAT'LL BE A HUNDRED LARGE.
NOW, ANYTHING ELSE I CAN DO FOR YOU?

WHAT CAN YOU TELL ME ABOUT THIS?

WELL, THE CUT IS JUST AWFUL. NO MEAT ON IT, EITHER. I GUESS YOU COULD BOIL IT AND SEE WHAT IT TASTES—
NO, UH, I MEANT, CAN YOU TELL ME WHAT THIS COMES FROM? I KNOW YOU DEAL IN THE EXOTICS... EVER SEEN THIS SORT OF MEAT BEFORE?

HMMM.

MAYBE... SNIFF, SNIFF...
YOU'RE NOT GOING TO LIKE THIS, THOUGH...

THE DOCKS.

HIDEKI TOJO,
GINSHU YAKUZA GANG.

MR. BUER? IS THAT YOU? WE HAVE THE, UH, MERCHANDISE YOU REQUESTED. SECOND BATCH, SAME NUMBER AND PRICE AS THE FIRST. ALL OVER 250 POUNDS.

EXCELLENT, MR. TOJO, EXCELLENT.

IF YOU DON'T MIND ME ASKING... WHAT EXACTLY ARE YOU GOING TO DO WITH THEM? WHY YOU ONLY WANT TUBBY ONES?

YOU'RE... GOING... TO... BOIL... THEM? RIGHT? OKAY...
I GUESS YOUR MONEY IS STILL AS GOOD AS ANYONE'S, BUT THAT'S SOME SICK SHIT, MISTER BUER, IF YOU DON'T MIND ME SAYING.
AH, YES, THE MONEY. I'M AFRAID OUR BUSINESS RELATIONSHIP IS NOW AT AN END, MISTER TOJO. I WON'T BE NEEDING ANY MORE SHIPMENTS AFTER THIS ONE. YOUR QUOTA IS FULFILLED.
AND PERSONALLY, I THINK YOU CHARGE A LITTLE TOO MUCH.

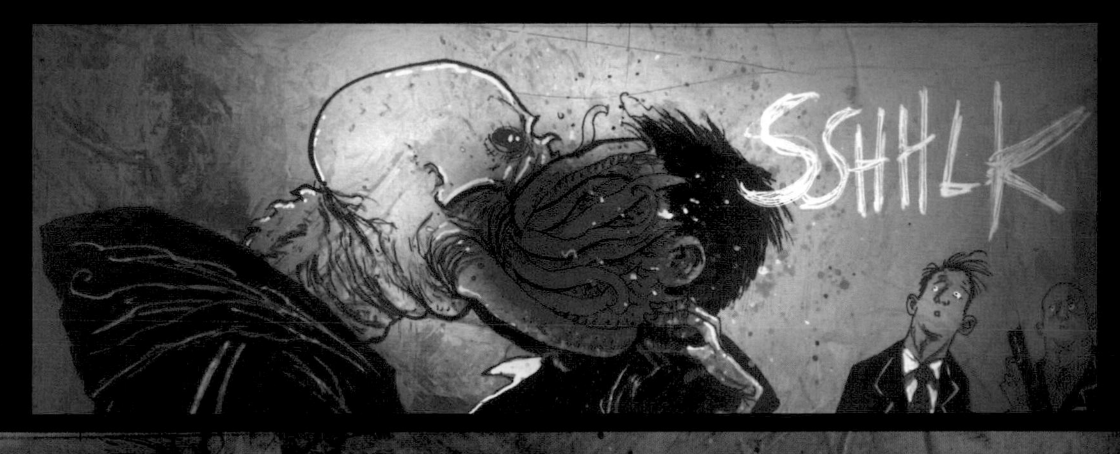
SSHLK

KILL THE REST.

Chapter 3

IT'S NOT EVERY DAY WE HAVE PRACTICALLY EVERY MEMBER OF THE GINSHU YAKUZA CRIME CLAN COME THROUGH THESE DOORS. ONE, MAYBE TWO, A YEAR—BUT TODAY, TWENTY-THREE.
I ALWAYS REMEMBER THEM. I WISH MORE OF MY CLIENTS WOULD MAKE MY LIFE MORE INTERESTING BY COVERING THEMSELVES IN PORNOGRAPHIC JAPANESE TATTOOS.

THE CLAN WERE TOUGH AS NAILS. MEANEST CREW THIS SIDE OF THE COUNTRY.
NOW, THEY'RE ALL LOOKING LIKE BUGS ON A WINDSHIELD. THIS HAS TO BE CONNECTED SOMEHOW TO THE OTHER DEATHS. THIS WAS NO GANG WAR.
FOR ONCE, YOU'RE RIGHT, TROTSKY. THOSE'RE BITE MARKS. THEY'RE NOT HUMAN. SOMETHING RATHER NASTY, PROBABLY WITH TENTACLES, DID THIS. GOT SOME SUCKER MARKS, TOO.
ERRR... WHAT DO YOU MEAN, TENTACLES?
IGNORE HIM. HE'S FOREIGN.

SO, WE'VE GOT TWENTY-THREE YAKUZA, AND ANOTHER FIVE REGULAR FOLK TONIGHT WHO LOOK LIKE THEY DIED FROM... INDIGESTION, SO TO SPEAK.
AND WE'VE FOUND MORE OF THOSE PILLS ON THE VICTIMS. LAB RESULTS POINT TO QUITE A FEW UNKNOWN COMPOUNDS. NOTHING WE'VE EVER SEEN BEFORE. IT'S VERY ODD.
THE NEAREST THING WE COULD LIKEN THEM TO, QUITE FRANKLY, IS ERECTILE DYSFUNCTION MEDICATION.
YOU'RE KIDDING.
SADLY, NO. ALL THE TESTS CONFIRM THE VICTIMS HAD TRACES OF IT IN THEIR BLOOD, ALL THROUGH THEIR BODIES, REALLY.
THEY'D ALL RECENTLY BEEN ENGAGED IN SEXUAL ACTIVITY. WHETHER IT WAS... UH, ALONE OR WITH SOMEONE, IT MADE NO DIFFERENCE.
BUT THEY ALL HAD BONERS?
WELL, IF YOU PUT IT THAT WAY, UH, THE MALES, YES. THE FEMALES...
WERE RECEIVING SOMETHING, SO TO SPEAK...

DO I NEED TO EXPLAIN TO YOU WHAT HAPPENS WHEN A MAN LOVES A LADY, WORM?
NO. I MEANT SOMETHING ELSE. THEY WERE BEING FERTILIZED...

UUHHH-HUH. ARE YOU *SURE* YOU HAVE A STRING OF EX-GIRLFRIENDS? MAYBE I'M GUESSING WHY THEY'RE EXES NOW? WHAT SORT OF BIOLOGY DID THEY TEACH IN WHATEVER THE HELL DIMENSION YOU'RE FROM?

NO, NOT WHAT I MEAN. I ASSURE YOU, I'M UP TO SPEED ON THE MATING HABITS OF HUMANS. EVEN THE ONES NOT IN THE VIDEOS.
I'LL HAVE YOU KNOW, I'VE BEEN DRINKING AND WENCHING WITH THE MARQUIS DE SADE BACK IN THE DAY. THAT CHAP KNEW HOW TO PARTY, IF YOU CATCH MY DRIFT. MAYBE SOMETIME I'LL—

DON'T MIND ME. I HAD THE LUCK TO BE BUILT WITHOUT THE NEED OF GELATINOUS, WOBBLY, PLEASURE-SEEKING BITS.
I DON'T RESENT NOT HAVING ANY AT ALL...
BLOODY HELL, PENDULUM.
YOU'RE GOING TO GO ON ABOUT THAT UNTIL I BLOODY PUPATE, AREN'T YOU?
WELL, MAYBE ONE DAY IF YOU'RE A GOOD CHAP, SANTA WORMWOOD WILL BRING YOU SOME NICE, BIG GENITALS ALL OF YOUR OWN. SO FOR NOW, WHY DON'T YOU SHUT UP ABOUT IT, EH?
ERRRR...
AHEM. SO, WORMY, YOU SAID THEY WERE BEING "FERTILIZED?"

AH, YES. BUT NOT IN THE USUAL WAY. NO, THOSE PILLS, I DO BELIEVE, ARE PART OF SOME LARGER IMPREGNATION PROCESS.
SOMETHING IN THEM IS SO FERTILE, IT IMPREGNATES AND GESTATES WITHIN ANY FEMALE THE MALE USER COMES INTO SWEATY, BUMPY LOVE WITH... OR... IF LEFT LONG ENOUGH, APPARENTLY THE MALE HIMSELF WILL DO AS A HOST.
IMPREGNATES THEM WITH WHAT?
I HAVE AN IDEA, BUT I'D STILL LIKE TO KNOW MORE. SAFE TO SAY YOU WON'T BE TAKING HAPPY SNAPS OR GIVING OUT CIGARS WHEN THE LITTLE BUNDLE OF JOY ARRIVES, THOUGH.

DEMON GRRLS

MASTABATORY EDITION

UUUUHH, I DON'T SUPPOSE YOU HAVE ANY OTHER COPIES OF THIS, DO YOU? IT'S JUST THAT IT GETS A BIT HARD AFTER THE FIFTEENTH TIME...

UUH UUH UHHH UHHH...
....UUUHHH... EEEEEEHH.... AWWWW....
...OOOOOO OOHHHH...
OKAY, ALL DONE. CAN I GET A CIGARETTE?
EXCELLENT, EXCELLENT! ALL I NEED FOR THE LAST BATCH.
AH, WHAT TIMING. HERE COME SOME MORE OF MY LOVELY CHILDREN. GATHER ROUND, CHILDREN! COME TO DADDY!

MR. TAMMUZ, I'M AFRAID YOUR WORK HERE IS DONE. TWELVE PINTS OF SEED WILL BE ALL I'LL BE NEEDING.
SO I'M AFRAID YOUR USEFULNESS IS NOW AT AN END.
CHILDREN, IF YOU PLEASE, DISPOSE OF YOUR BIOLOGICAL FATHER.
UUUH, YOU PROMISED ME...
NOOAAARRRGH!
NEARLY THERE. YOUR NUMBER AND ENERGY GROWS WITH EACH PASSING MOMENT. THE CIRCLE IS ALMOST COMPLETE. SOON, MY CHILDREN, SOOOOON.

SO, LET ME GET THIS STRAIGHT...

...YOU'RE GOING TO TEST THE PILLS ON YOURSELF? I HOPE YOU'RE NOT EXPECTING ME TO BE... INVOLVED.

WELL I WOULDN'T SAY NO... AHEM... BUT YES, YES I AM. NOW HOLD ON.

GULP

NOW, WATCH AND WAIT. I THINK I'M ABOUT TO BECOME A DADDY.
JESUS.

SPONTANEOUS CONCEPTION
etc etc
I'M GOING TO BE AN UNCLE.

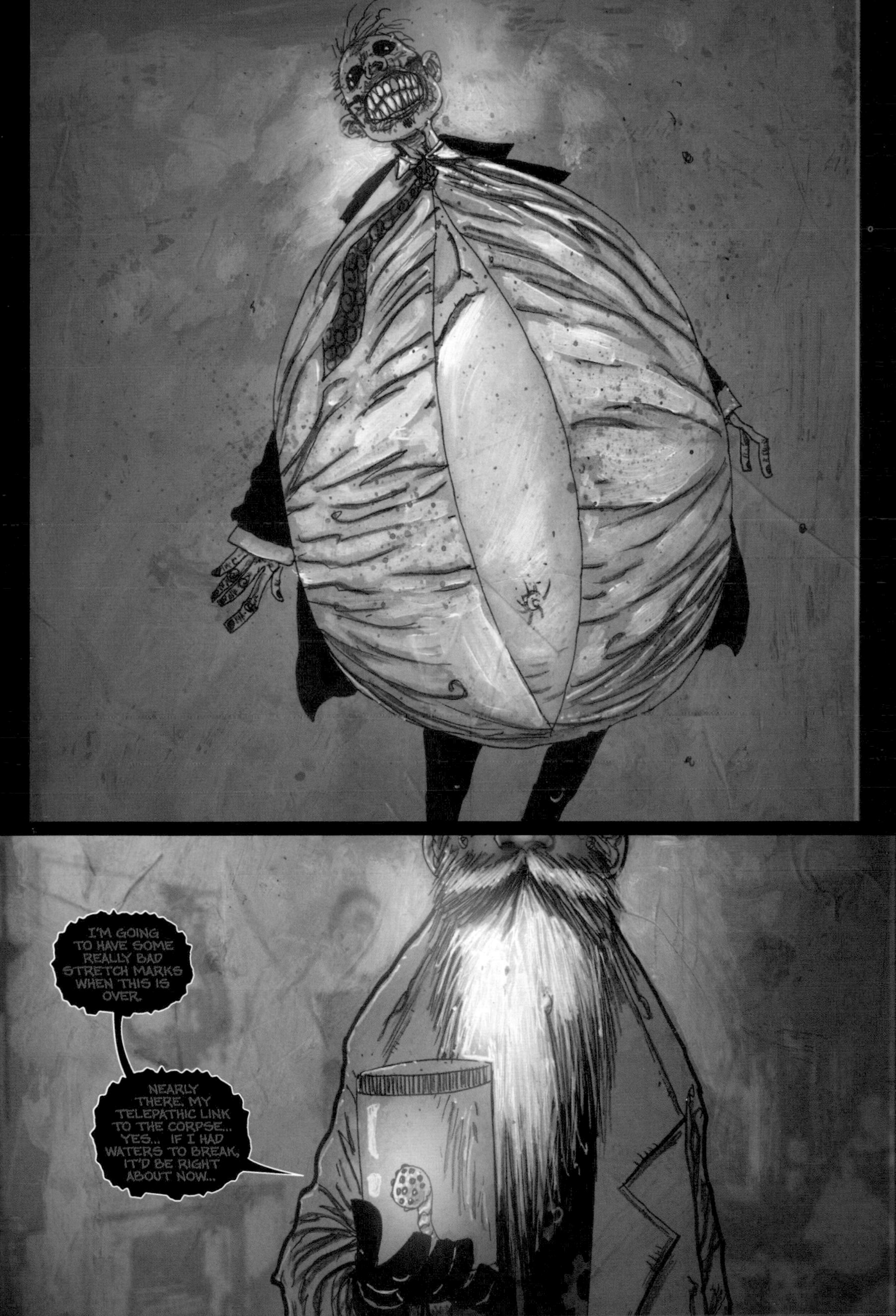
I'M GOING TO HAVE SOME REALLY BAD STRETCH MARKS WHEN THIS IS OVER.
NEARLY THERE, MY TELEPATHIC LINK TO THE CORPSE... YES... IF I HAD WATERS TO BREAK, IT'D BE RIGHT ABOUT NOW...

BACK AT BUER'S PLACE...

THAT'S IT SNOOKIES, COME HERE... THAAAAAT'S IT...

SO PRETTY. YOU WILL SERVE YOUR PURPOSE WELL. DADDY LOVES YOU VERY MUCH.

(tender moment)

licky licky

PLEASE... PLEASE... DON'T BOIL ME LIKE THE OTHERS...

AH, YOU SPEAK! YOU'RE IN LUCK, HUMAN. I WON'T BE NEEDING YOUR BODY FAT. I THINK I'VE MADE MY LAST BATCH.

BESIDES, YOU'VE LOST SO MUCH WEIGHT YOU COULD PROBABLY FIT THROUGH THE BARS SOON?

OH, THANK GOD... THANK GOD.
NO, YOU'LL MAKE AN EXCELLENT LAST MEAL FOR MY RAVENOUS BROOD. PLENTY OF MEAT STILL ON YOU. COULDN'T LET THAT GO TO WASTE, NOW COULD WE?

FEAST, MY CHILDREN. YOU'LL NEED ALL YOUR STRENGTH FOR WHAT IS TO COME!
NOOO!
I CAN FEEL IT... I CAN FEEL IT... CHILDREN... THE DARK ENERGY IS RISING...
MUNCH
MUNCH
CRUNK
MONCH
THE LAST OF YOUR BROTHERS AND SISTERS ARE BEING BORN INTO THIS WORLD AT THIS VERY MOMENT. PREPARE YOURSELVES—THE TIME IS NEARLY UPON US!

LOOK AT THAT. MY BACK MUST BE KILLING ME, THERE.
I AM SO NEVER HAVING KIDS.
ME, NEITHER.
SHUT UP.
WORM, YOU'RE BURSTING!
THANK YOU. I HAVE EYES, YOU KNOW. TWENTY OF THEM.

OKAY, REMEMBER WHAT TO DO? THE ROPE! THE ROPE!
WHOP WHOP
THAT'S IT... GENTLY...

YOU'RE SURE ABOUT THIS?
SNATCH!
YES, YES. HURRY AND TIE ME UP BEFORE IT BOLTS.
OKAY, WE'RE OFF. MY TELEPATHIC LINK TO MY HUSK OF A BODY MEANS WE SHOULD BE ABLE TO TRACK IT TO ITS NEST. I SUGGEST YOU BRING GUNS. LOTS OF GUNS.
YEAH. KINDA FIGURED THAT ONE OUT.

THOK THOK THOK

THOK

OW. THAT ONE HURT.

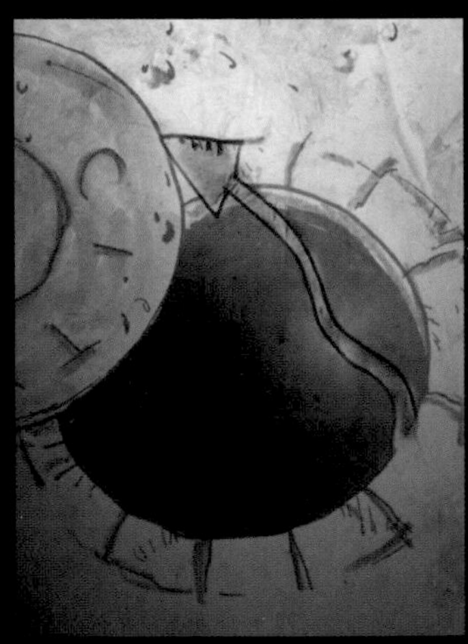

THUMMP

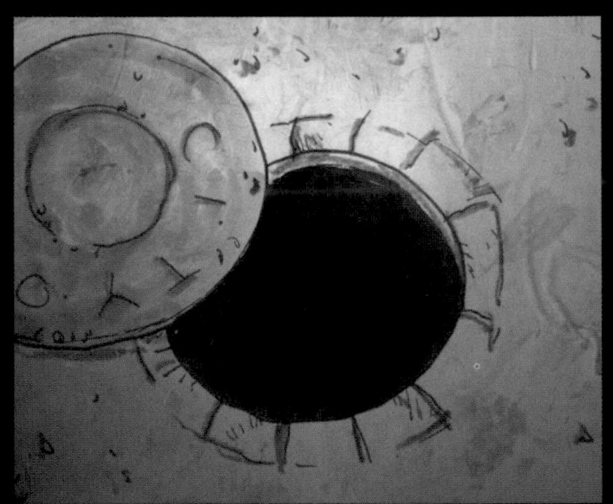

HMMM... WHY IS IT ALWAYS IN THE BLOODY SEWERS?

YES, MY CHILDREN... SING.... SING YOUR DARK SONG SO THAT *HE* MAY HEAR YOU... YOUR CIRCLE IS NEARLY COMPLETE!

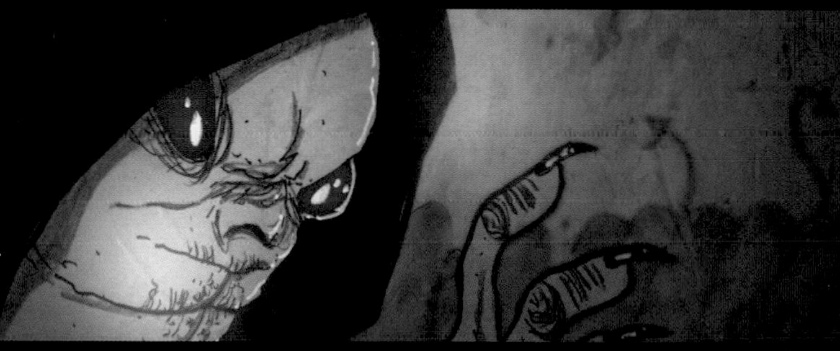

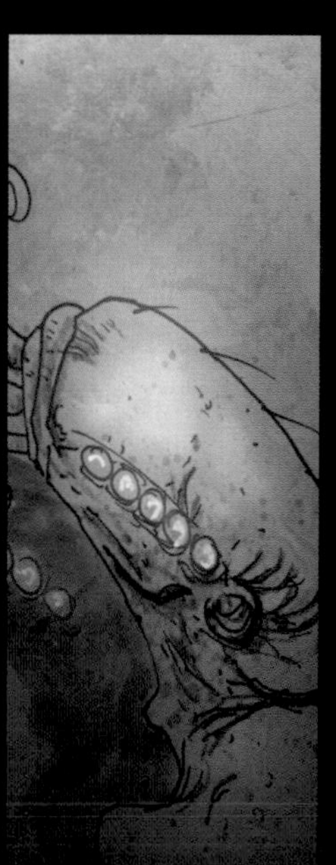

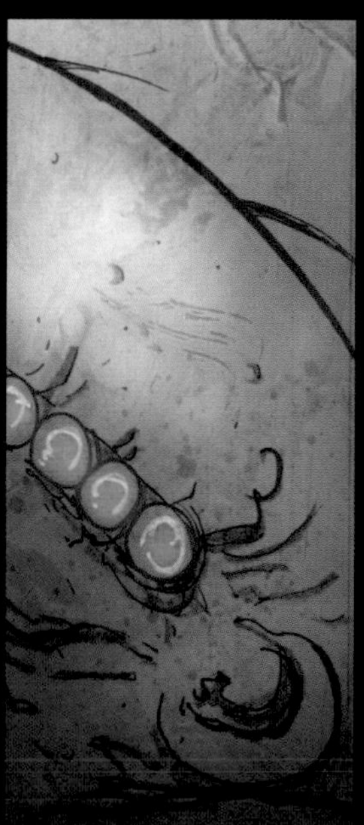

THE FINAL PIECE... EH? WHAT IS THIS?

YOU ARE THE LAST. THE LAST KEY I NEED TO TURN THE LOCK.

BEAUTIFUL.

THIS IS SO HUMILIATING... SIGH.

SHLP SHLP SHLP SALP SALP etc.

A CORPSE. A WELL-DRESSED CORPSE. YOU CAME FROM THIS, MY PRETTY? HOW ODD. HUMAN SEXUAL ACTS NEVER CEASE TO AMAZE ME IN THEIR... DEVIANCY.

NEVER MIND... THE CIRCLE IS COMPLETE. NOW, FOR SACRIFICE!

OOOH, I'M GOING TO NEED STITCHING.

WHAT?

KER-
CHAK
OH, ALLO, OLD CHAP. WHAT'RE YOU UP TO, THEN?

Chapter 4

I'M SORRY... WHAT?
WHO ARE YOU? HOW DARE YOU ENTER MY SANCTUARY? AND AT THIS CRITICAL TIME, NO LESS!
CRITICAL, EH? SOUNDS LIKE THAT TIME OF THE MONTH TO ME... IF I COULD FIGURE OUT WHAT SEX YOU ARE.

WHAT ARE YOU, TIN MAN? WHAT MAGIKS HAVE BROUGHT YOU TO LIFE?
THAT'S CLOCKWORK TIN MAN TO YOU, PAL.
YES, YES, ERM, SPEAKING OF MAGIC... WHAT'S ALL THIS IN AID OF, THEN? LOOKS TO ME LIKE YOU'RE HAVING A BIT OF A PARTY BUT I DON'T MUCH LIKE YOUR GUESTS.
MY CHILDREN? THEY ARE BEAUTIFUL!
WELL, IN FAIRNESS, I'VE WOKEN UP NEXT TO WORSE, BUT THAT'S NOT THE POINT. YOU CAN'T GO SPAWNING THESE THINGS OUT OF INNOCENT HUMAN WOMBS WITHOUT THEIR PERMISSION. IT'S JUST NOT DONE. GIVES THEM A RATHER BAD CASE OF INSTANT DEATH, IT DOES.
JUST WHO ARE YOU, CORPSE? WHO ARE YOU TO PRESUME TO TELL ME WHAT TO DO?

I'M WORMWOOD.
AND YOU HAVE THE WORST CASE OF PLUMBER'S CRACK FOR A FACE I'VE EVER SEEN.
NEVER HEARD OF YOU.
AND NOW NO ONE ELSE EVER WILL.

BEHOLD, I AM BUER, DEMON OF THE SECOND ORDER, COMMANDER OF FIFTY LEGIONS OF HELL!
BOOM
BOOM
BOOM
OH, WONDERFUL. THAT'D MAKE YOU FROM THE XION-GHATAR DIMENSION. YOU GUYS ARE LIKE FARTS IN AN ELEVATOR.
YOU KNOW, I WOKE UP THIS MORNING THINKING "WELL, TODAY I'D LIKE TO FIGHT FOR MY LIFE AGAINST LARGE BLUE MAGIC ENERGY TENTACLES OR SOME SUCH."

BEGIN, MY CHILDREN! YOUR TIME IS NOW!
USE YOUR ENERGIES! OPEN THE GATEWAY!
GATEWAY?
BLAM
OH, YES, GATEWAY. BLOODY FOOL IS GOING TO USE THOSE THINGS AS AN ENERGY SOURCE TO OPEN A TEMPORARY AND HIGHLY ILLEGAL DIMENSIONAL GATE.
SHOULD HAVE REALIZED.

YES, CORPSE. A GATE. THROUGH WHICH COMES YOUR DOOM.

QUITE THE DRAMA QUEEN, I SEE.

I HAVE TOILED FOR MONTHS, GROWING MY CHILDREN FOR THIS DAY. MY SACRIFICIAL LAMBS WILL GIVE ME THE ENERGY I NEED TO BRIDGE THE WORLDS. DO YOU KNOW HOW HARD IT WAS TO FIND THAT MANY WILLING INCUBATORS?

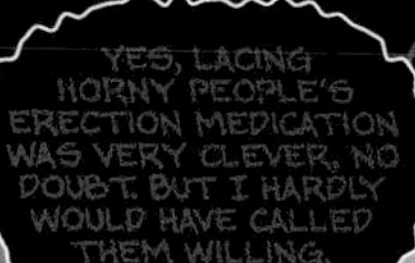

OK, SQUIDY...
JUST WHAT'RE YOU TRYING TO PULL THROUGH THAT GATE, THEN? TELL ME!
WHY, IT IS MALOCH. PRINCE OF THE LAND OF TEARS. HE PROMISES ME POWER AND DOMINION OVER THIS WORLD ONCE HE HAS HAD HIS WAY WITH HER... UURRK!
MALOCH? WELL, THERE WON'T BE MUCH OF A WORLD LEFT AFTER HE EATS THE BLOODY THING.
WE'VE GOT TO STOP IT BEFORE THE GATE OPENS OR—

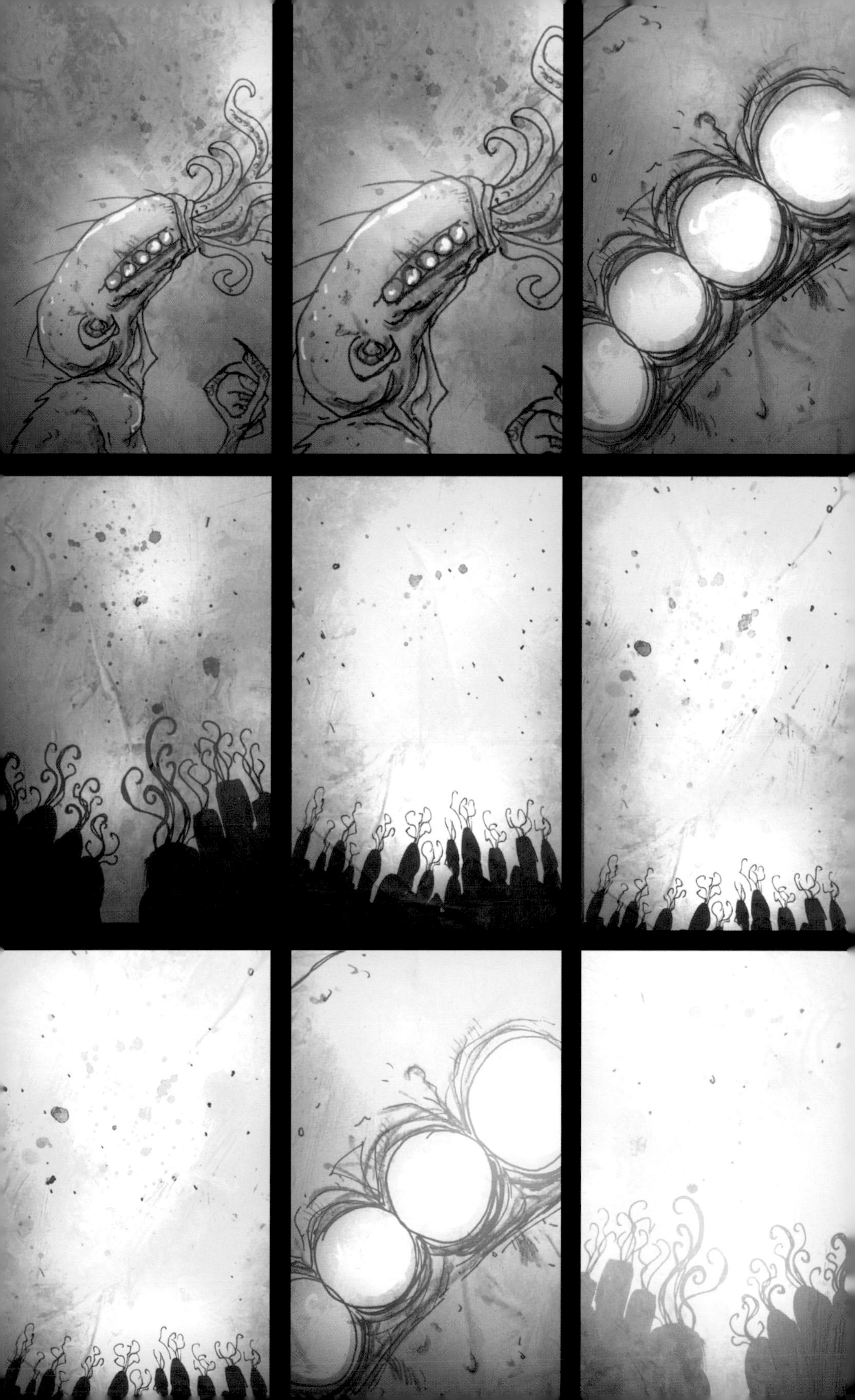

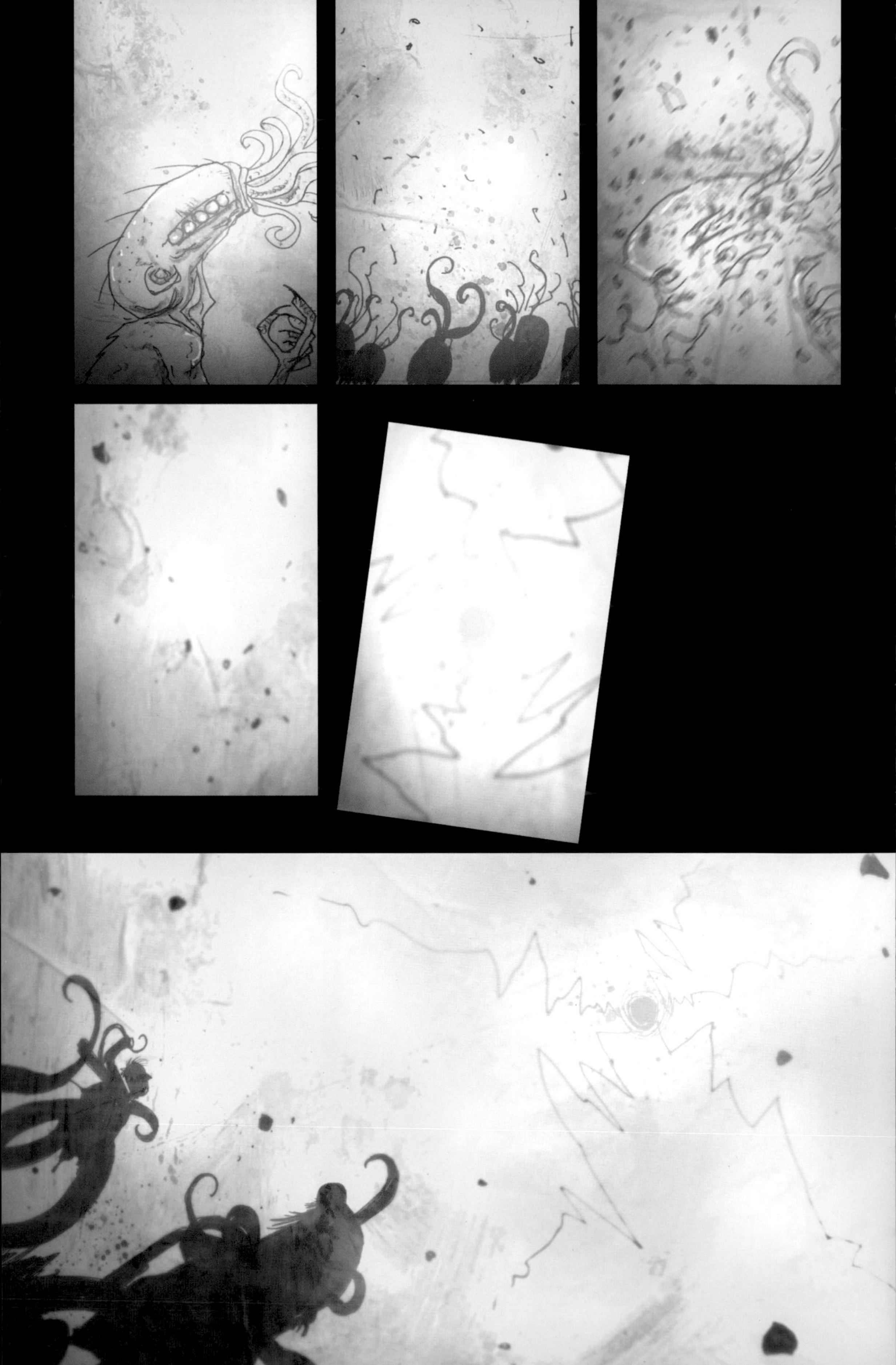

BUGGER.

MASTER! YOU HAVE COME!

TREMBLE, BEINGS OF THIS WORLD, FOR YOUR FINAL MOMENTS ARE AT HAND.

MASTER?

KRRRRRK
PENDULUM! TIME TO PUT YOURSELF IN SECOND GEAR, OLD CHAP.
BOOM
BOOM
CLIK
SIGH.
click click
OK.
WHZZZZ
BRKK
CHKt
CHKt
Whrrrr
LET'S MAKE SANDWICHES.
HEY, I DIDN'T KNOW HE COULD DO THAT!
BUT OF COURSE. I MADE HIM. AND PROPERLY, AT THAT.

CERTIFIED BATTLE-GRADE EXOSKELETAL SYSTEMS. MAGNUS FIVE COHESION AND CO-ORDINATION CHIPS.

SOKK

NINTH-GENERATION DUAL PROCESSING CONFLICT RESOLUTION HYDRAULICS SYSTEMS. POWERFUL ENOUGH TO TAKE DOWN A SIXTH-SPHERE ARCH DAEMON.

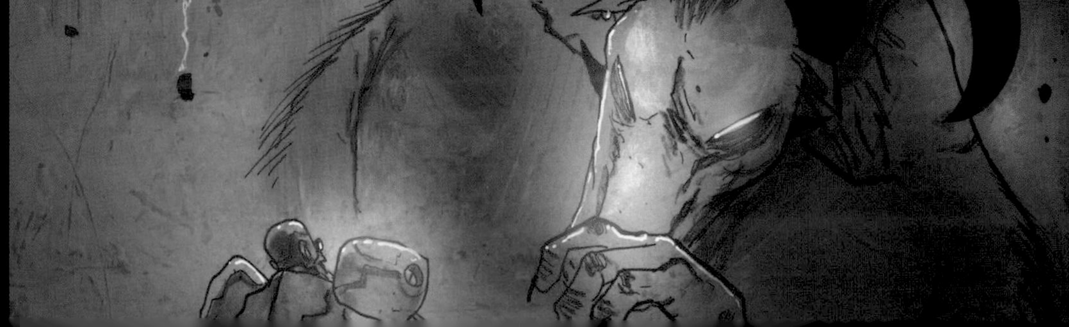

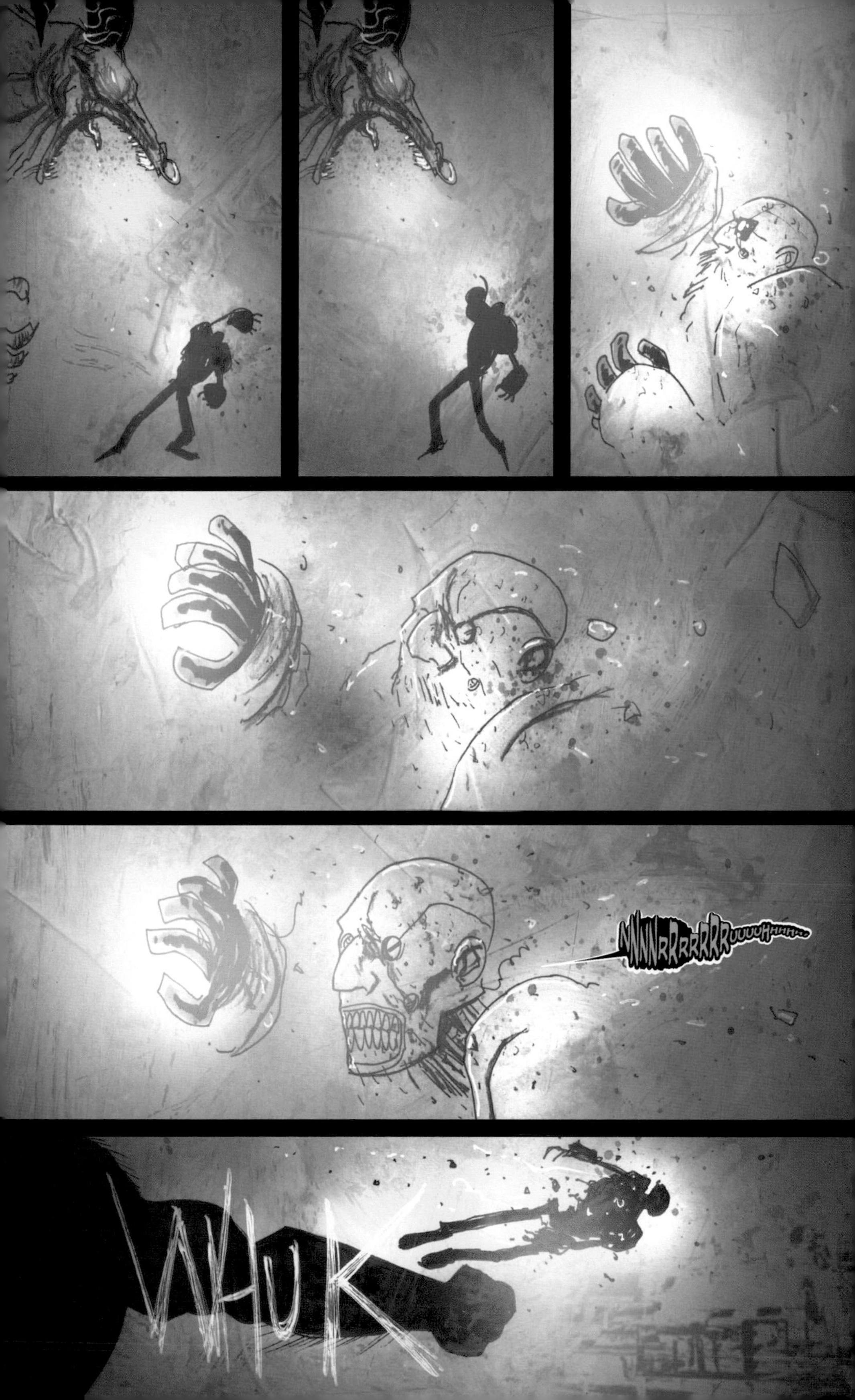
NNNNRRRRRRRUUUUHHHH..
WHUK

ALL OF WHICH APPARENTLY MEANS HE'LL LAST ABOUT FIVE SECONDS AGAINST THIS GUY.
KRNCH

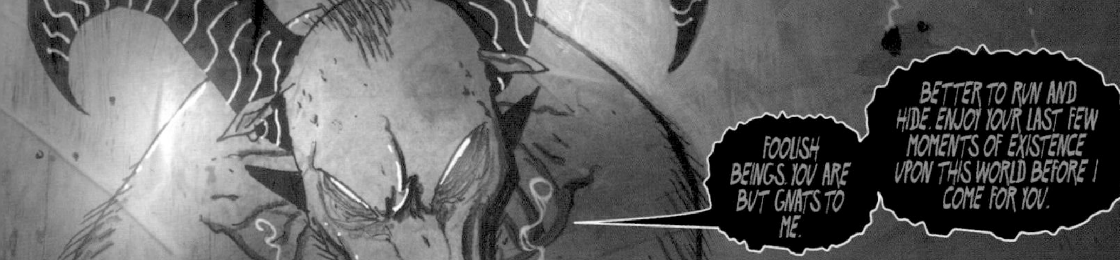

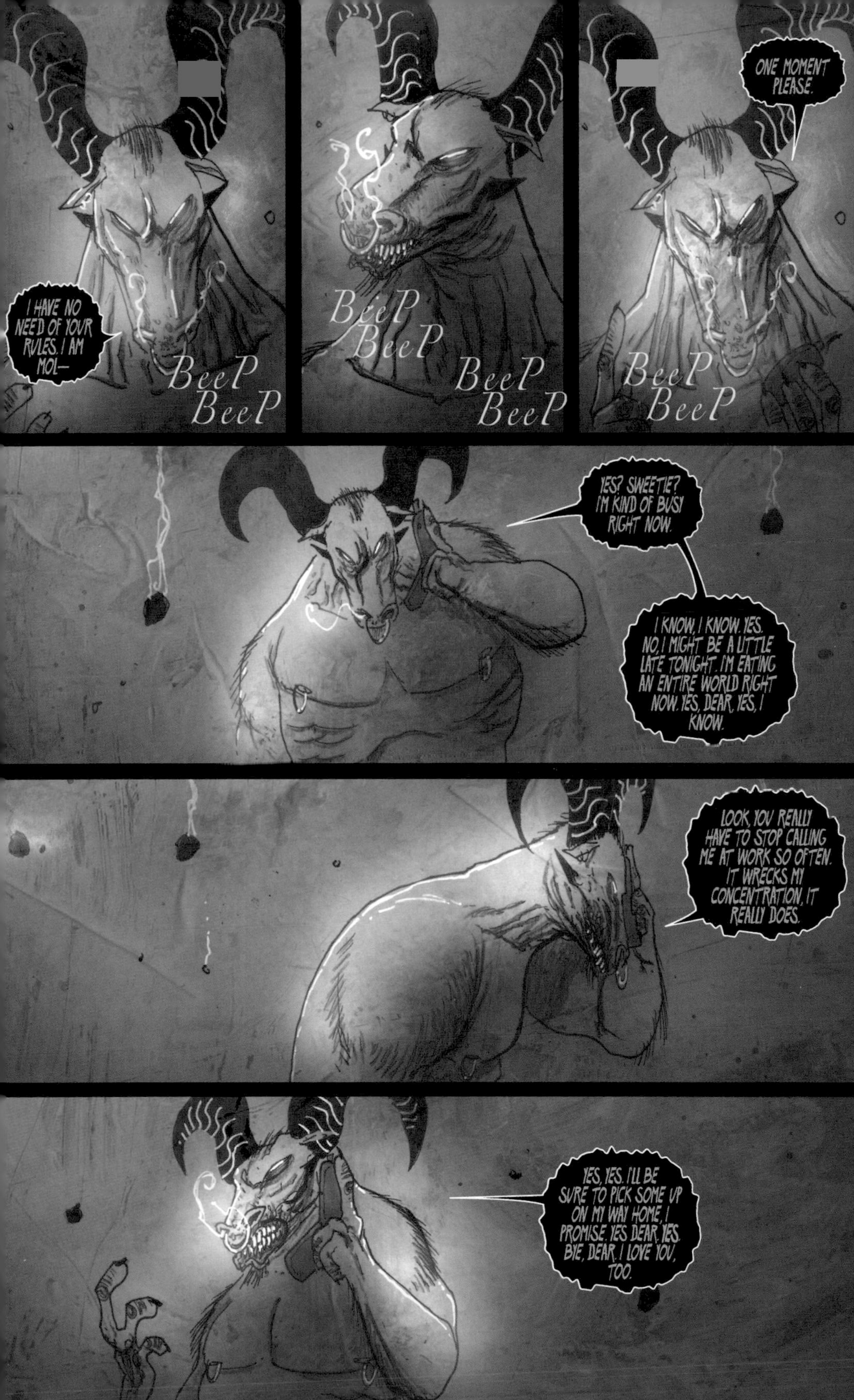
I HAVE NO NEED OF YOUR RULES. I AM MOL—
BeeP BeeP
BeeP BeeP
BeeP BeeP
ONE MOMENT PLEASE.
BeeP BeeP
YES? SWEETIE? I'M KIND OF BUSY RIGHT NOW.
I KNOW, I KNOW. YES. NO, I MIGHT BE A LITTLE LATE TONIGHT. I'M EATING AN ENTIRE WORLD RIGHT NOW. YES, DEAR, YES, I KNOW.
LOOK, YOU REALLY HAVE TO STOP CALLING ME AT WORK SO OFTEN. IT WRECKS MY CONCENTRATION, IT REALLY DOES.
YES, YES. I'LL BE SURE TO PICK SOME UP ON MY WAY HOME, I PROMISE. YES DEAR. YES. BYE, DEAR. I LOVE YOU, TOO.

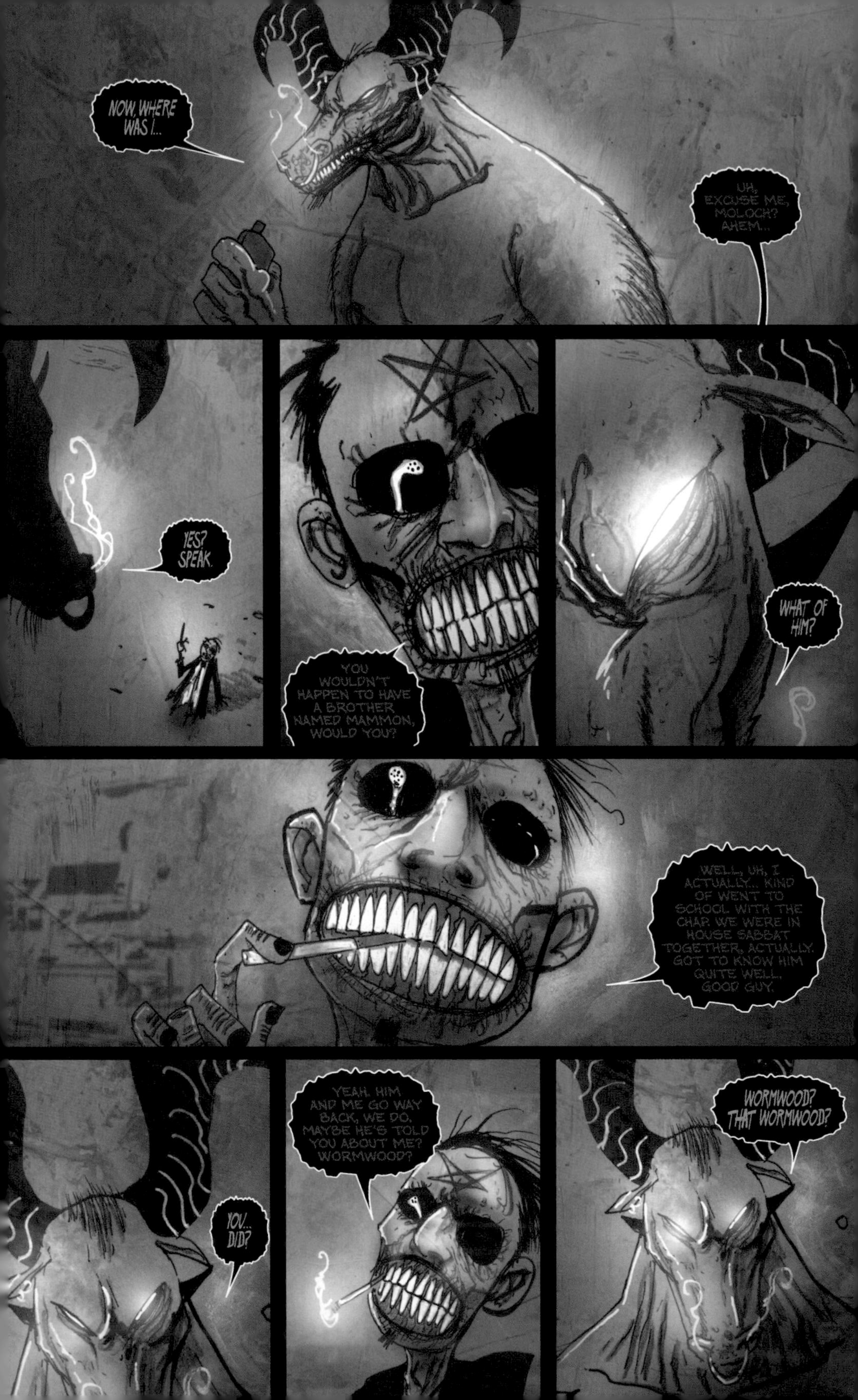

NOW, WHERE WAS I...
UH, EXCUSE ME, MOLOCH? AHEM...
YES? SPEAK.
YOU WOULDN'T HAPPEN TO HAVE A BROTHER NAMED MAMMON, WOULD YOU?
WHAT OF HIM?

DAMN, MAN! YEAH, MAMMON MENTIONS YOU ALL THE TIME! JEEZ, I TELL YOU, SOME OF THOSE STORIES...

SORRY I DIDN'T RECOGNIZE YOU THERE. WHAT WITH THE NEW BODY AND ALL

YEAH, SORRY ABOUT THAT. I TEND TO SWAP THEM AROUND EVERY NOW AND THEN.

SO, UH, WHAT'S UP?

WELL, OLD CHAP, I WAS KIND OF WONDERING IF MAYBE YOU WOULDN'T MIND NOT EATING AND DESTROYING THIS DIMENSION. I SORT OF CALL IT HOME THESE DAYS AND IT JUST WOULDN'T BE THE SAME IF EVERYONE WAS WITHOUT THEIR SKIN AND SCREAMING AND SUCH, YOU KNOW?

WELL, I GUESS I'LL CALL IT A DAY, THEN.

CAN'T SAY HOW SORRY I AM. GOD, I MUST APPEAR LIKE SUCH A RUDE PRICK.

OH, DON'T WORRY ABOUT IT. IT'S SORTED NOW. GIVE MY REGARDS TO YOUR BROTHER NEXT TIME YOU SEE HIM, WILL YOU? TELL HIM I'VE NOT FORGOTTEN THAT FIVER HE OWES ME, EITHER!

HEH, WILL DO. YOU KNOW, WE HAVE A FAMILY GATHERING COMING UP. YOU SHOULD DROP ON BY AND SHARE SOME STORIES. ALL OF MAMMON'S ARE GETTING A LITTLE OLD.

SO, THAT'S IT?
YUP, THAT'S IT.
YOUR CASE IS SOLVED, TROTSKY, AND HEY LOOK, I'VE SAVED THE WORLD. AGAIN. OH, AND I'VE BEEN RIPPED ASUNDER. AGAIN. AND DO I HEAR A THANK YOU FROM YOU?
...
THANK YOU.
HiSSSSSS
RIGHT, THEN. WHO'S GOING TO GIVE ME A LIFT?
I THINK I LIKE YOU, OH, YES.

PENDULUM! WHERE ARE YOU? WE'RE GOING HOME. GET A MOVE ON, I NEED A PINT.
SURE, NO PROBLEM.
I'M FINE.
I'M GOING TO HAVE WORDS WITH MEDUSA ABOUT HOW THAT BUGR CHAP WAS ABLE TO GET THROUGH THE DIMENSIONAL GATE IN THE FIRST PLACE. STANDARDS MEAN NOTHING THESE DAYS, I TELL YOU.

COME ON, LET'S GO HOME.
MAYBE EVEN SEE ABOUT YOUR BITS, EH?
YOU MEAN IT? YOU REALLY MEAN IT?
WE'LL SEE. FIRST I NEED MY BLOODY LEGS BACK, DON'T I?

Covers

ALLO.
© Templesmith

templesmith
2006

© TEMPLESMITH

Templesmith

Templesmith2006

Templesmith
2006

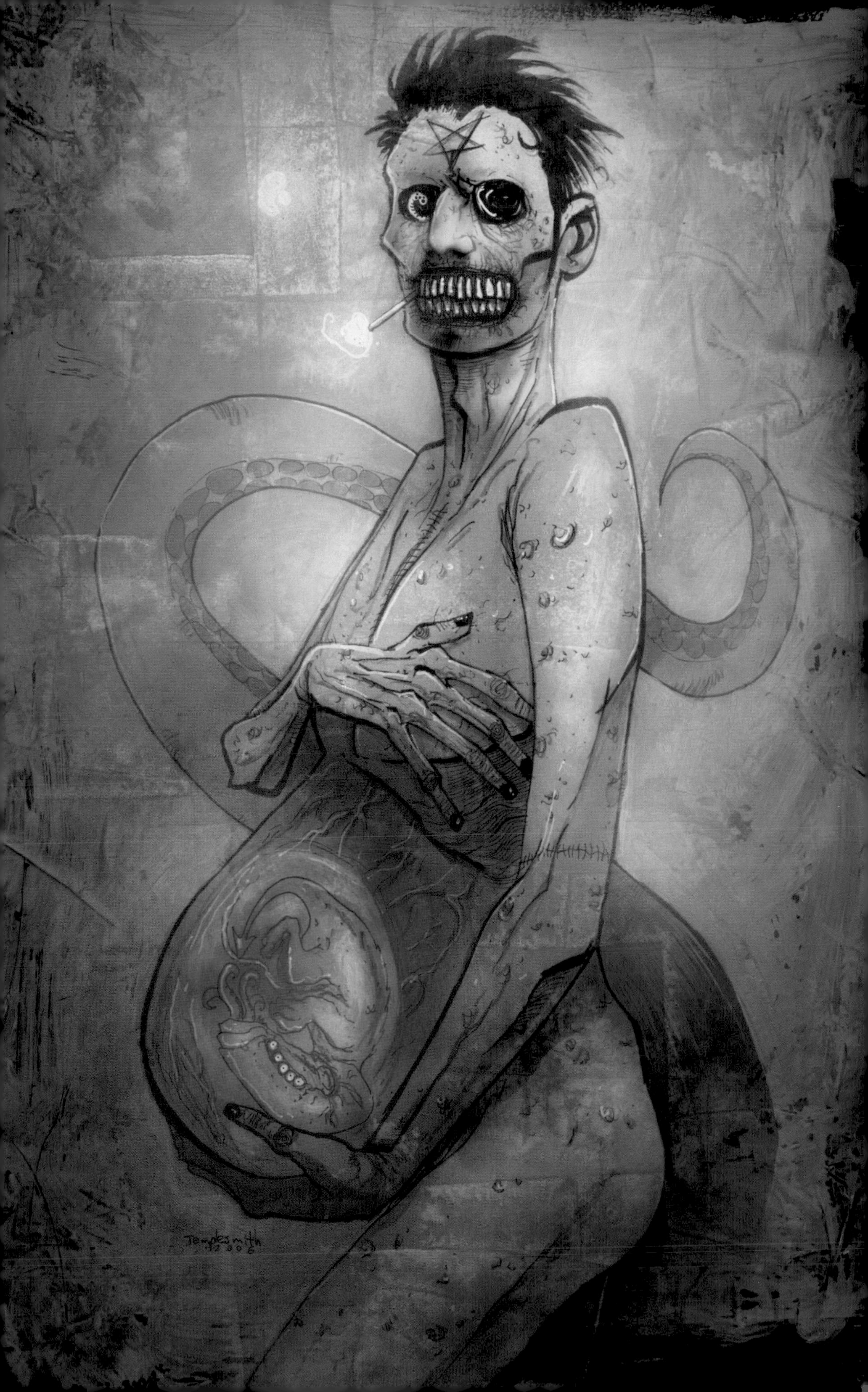
Templesmith
2006

Templesmith2006

templesmith2006

voodoo lady
TEMPLESMITH
2006

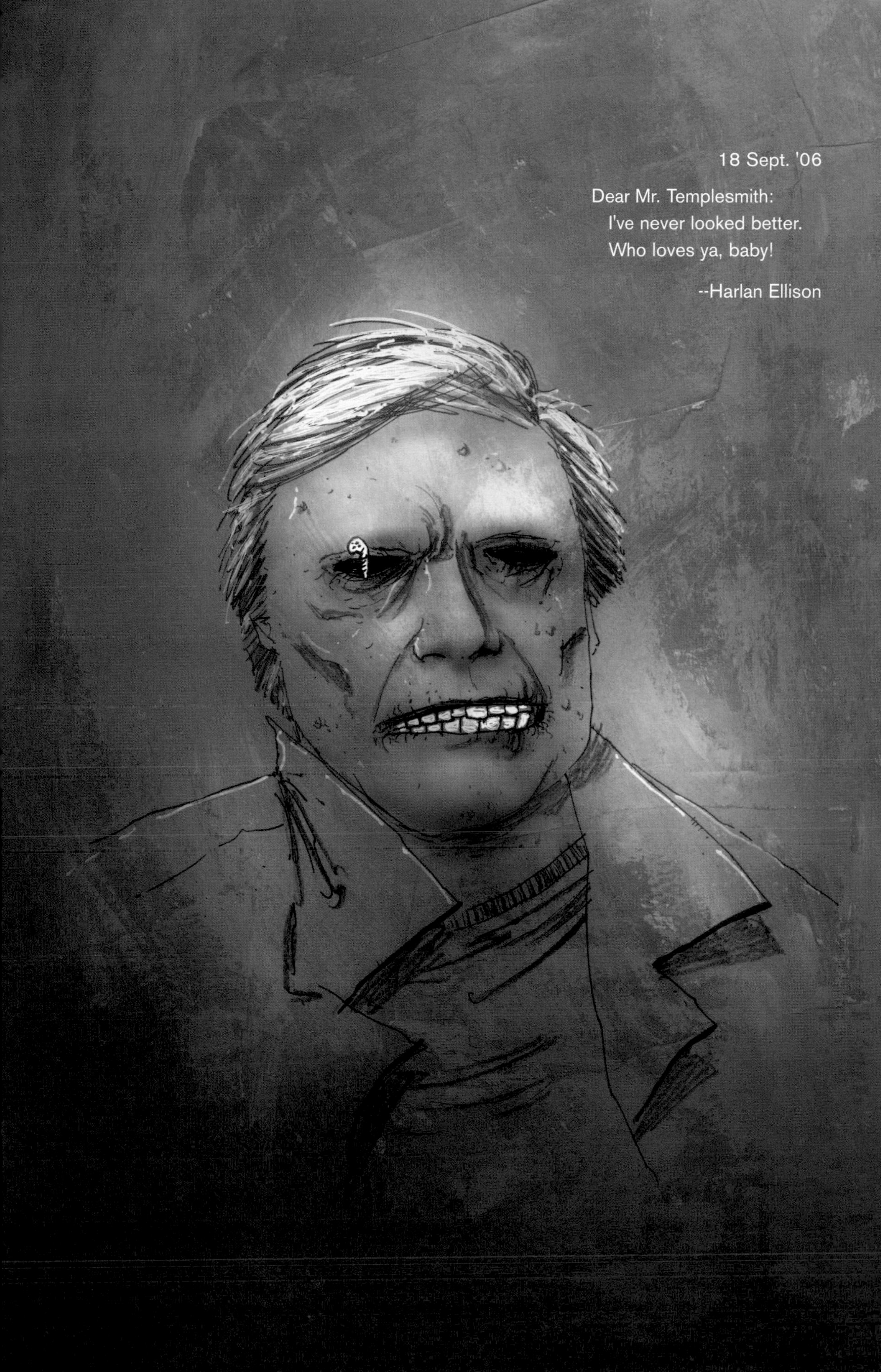
18 Sept. '06
Dear Mr. Templesmith:
I've never looked better.
Who loves ya, baby!
--Harlan Ellison

Sketchbook

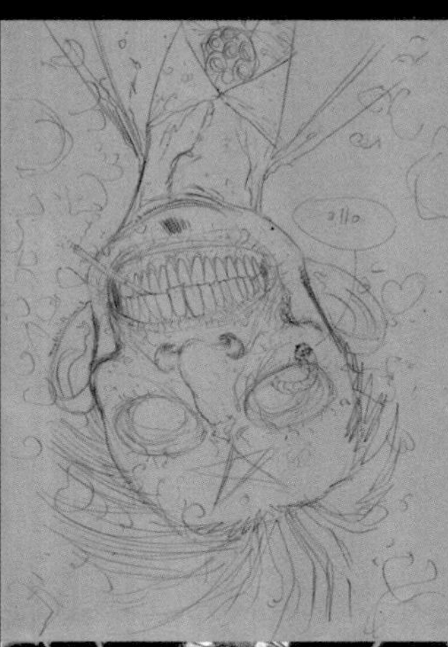

I get asked how I do my art an awful lot but there's really not much I can say other than, "I work with layers and stuff about in Photoshop over existing scanned in hand drawn images." Or something like that.

The process seems to change all the time and I'm trying to do more and more in the real world, (when everyone else seems to be doing the opposite!) probably partly in response to critics who think you just press a button and out comes something similar to the Sistine Chapel.

I wish it were that easy.

Anyways, here's a bunch of shots showing how the cover for issue #0 evolved, from sketch on tinted paper, to ink and paint, to scan, layering and coloring in Photoshop...

...I can't really talk about filters, since I really steer away from them. My general Photoshop method barely, if ever, involves actual "drawing on the computer." Yet. All real world textures and photos.

As for the actual PS process, I'm not really going to say much, since if you want to learn and evolve as an artist, you have to find your own way and tinker with your tools. It's the best path to learning and finding your own voice!*

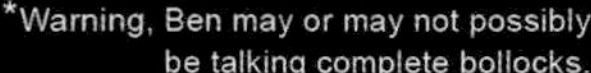

*Warning, Ben may or may not possibly be talking complete bollocks.

From thumbnail to finished page

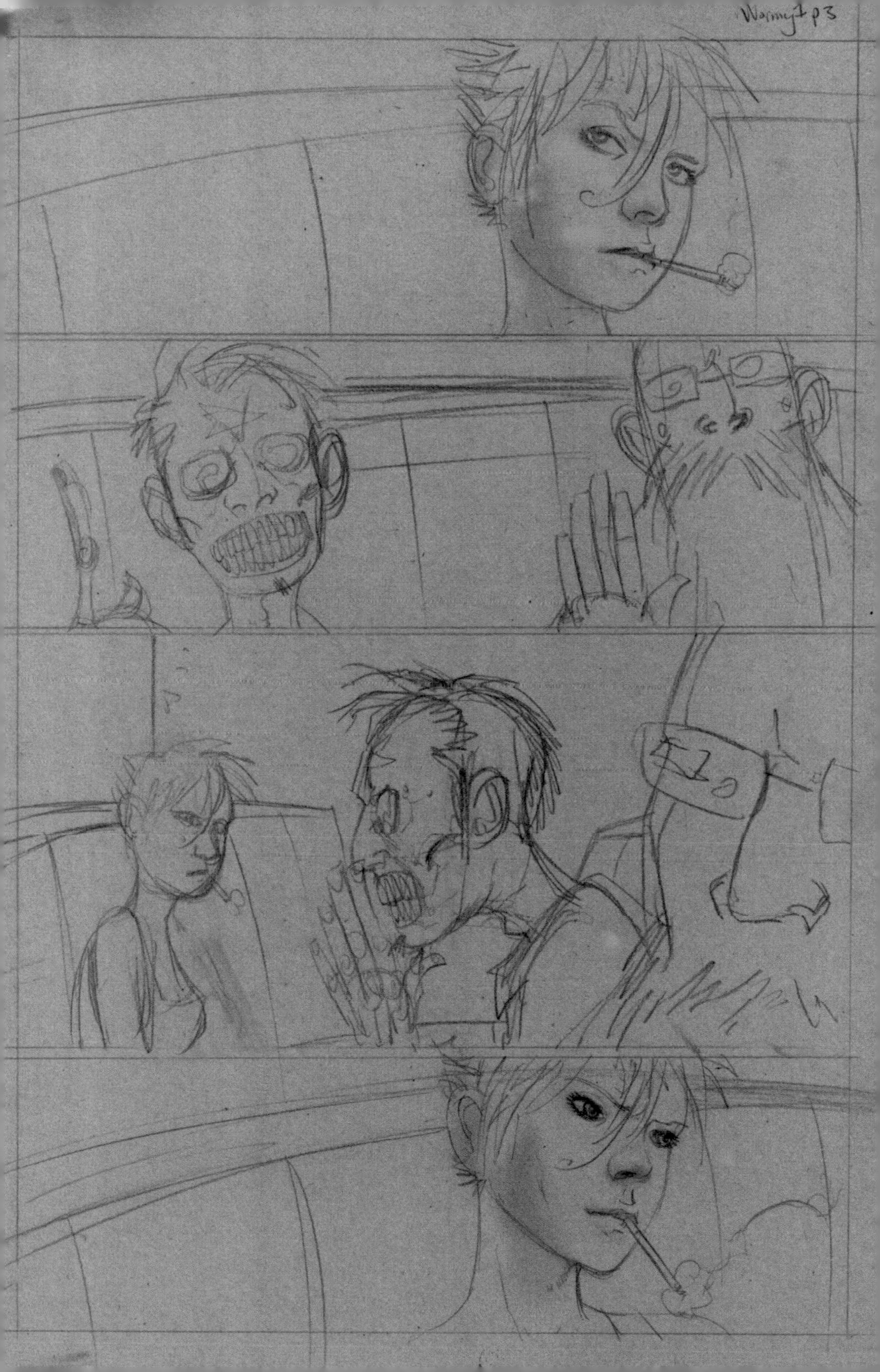
Warmy1 p3

Pinup Gallery

A.J. CASPERITE 2006
pinup by A.J. Casperite
www.artwanted.com/ajcasperite
WORMWOOD

pinup by Colton Worley
www.worleyart.com
blog :artistcoltonworley.blogspot.com
e-mail: coltonworley@yahoo.com

pinup by Grant Gould
www.grantgould.com

pinup by Aadijin, colors by BT
www.aadisalman.com

Wormwood, by the multi talented Art Grafunkel

Ben Templesmith |

Born in 1978, Ben hails from Perth, Australia.

As a commercial illustrator his most notable works are the Eisner award nominated *30 Days of Night* and *Fell*. He has also worked on *Star Wars, Army of Darkness, Silent Hill* and *Buffy The Vampire Slayer* properties along with artwork for music bands and concept art for movies.

These days Ben lives and works in his studio in Perth where he attempts in vain to get what those in the "industry" call "sleep" at least a couple hours a day. There's also a strange American lurking about his home, although she could easily be a figment of a caffeine-induced delirium.